Calling on the power of the feminine to correct the disharmony of our times, the author seeks to galvanize the female spirit to act out its cosmic blueprint as peacekeeper, nurturer and creative force against encroaching mechanistic (Yang) influences. This book explores the full power of the true feminine against the dominance of patriarchy, invoking personal responsibility in every woman. Its message is a compassionate and compelling appeal to create a better and fulfilling future. Well worth reading as an inspiration for all women.

**Krysia Gallien**, is the founder(1980) of the Center for Creative Being in Montreal, Canada. She is a certified yoga instructor, teacher  and a Polarity therapist with a private practice. For over 25 years she has been giving workshops and classes  in the healing arts to encourage the unfolding of new spiritual consciousness in women.

Corrine write with passion and backs her findings with extensive research. Her book is for the serious reader (primarily woman) who is ready to be inspired and take on the responsibility of effective positive change to heighten world consciousness. I enjoyed reading this book.

**Selwa Hamati**, lives in California, United States. She is a Neuro-Linguistic-Programming Practicioner and Hypnotherapist and is a certified member of the Association for Integrative Psychology. She is also the author of published books such as *Once Upon a Recession* and *7 Keys to Freedom*

*Womanity's Cosmic Blueprint* is a fine and well researched book. Its intent, form the beginning, is to remind all women to activate themselves at this time to settle accelerating world problems that threaten our survival. The author prompts women to come together in passionate force to resolve the still serious, negative attitudes against their gender and move that force into creating a healthy humanity. A good read to raise consciousness

**Suzanne Price**, is the author of *Death and the World of In Between* (2012). She was also for many years  the  group leader of studies and secretary for the Montreal, Canada, branch of the Theosophical Society, a worldwide organization focused on pursuing higher truths beyond religion.

# Womanity's Cosmic Blueprint

woman of the earth-hearth-heart

# Womanity's Cosmic Blueprint

woman of the earth-hearth-heart

## Corinne Carmen

AXIS MUNDI
BOOKS

Winchester, UK
Washington, USA

First published by Axis Mundi Books, 2014
Axis Mundi Books is an imprint of John Hunt Publishing Ltd., Laurel House, Station Approach,
Alresford, Hants, SO24 9JH, UK
office1@jhpbooks.net
www.johnhuntpublishing.com
www.axismundi-books.com

For distributor details and how to order please visit the 'Ordering' section on our website.

Text copyright: Corinne Carmen 2013

ISBN: 978 1 78279 321 2

A CIP catalogue record for this book is available from the British Library.

Design: Stuart Davies
www.stuartdaviesart.com

Printed in the USA by Edwards Brothers Malloy

We operate a distinctive and ethical publishing philosophy in all
areas of our business, from our global network of authors to
production and worldwide distribution.

# CONTENTS

Dedication

To all the females I have known and admire that
are TOTAL women.
Thank you for enriching my life and mirroring to me the
diversity and depth of my own womanness.

"Things do not change; we do."
Henry David Thoreau


This book will reconnect lost woman with her cosmic identity, hopefully initiating metamorphosis back to the *TRUE* self.

# Preface

It is one thing to come to understand enlightening information that raises us up from our ignorance. We are always learning, for life is our teacher and the planet is our schoolroom. After all, that is why we are here. You might say, as you pick up this book, that you have already read many others written about the Goddess or feminine principle. I see those as the preliminary texts that have allowed the public to gradually learn about Her energy that demands acknowledgement. Change, however, requires more than learning about something. We can stop at knowledge or we can mobilize it by acting upon it to create a new reality. In other words, understanding is the first step; knowing within that this information is true is step two; and then finally manifesting this truth through action is the third.

Womanity's Cosmic Blueprint encourages women to once and for all become the spiritual warriors that fully embrace and materialize the Feminine Consciousness as per the Universes' plan-in-waiting. In this eleventh hour as humanity, all life and the planet teeter on extinction, action or step three is *now* required.

Enjoy this journey and its revelations.
Corinne Carmen

# Introduction

This is not another book about the feminist movement nor does it take a superiority stance, uplifting woman while degrading man. Rather, it attempts to direct woman back to her seed of identity, to her core being. This seed within, holds the deepest mysteries that define *TRUE* woman, and is her cosmic blueprint. Finding it opens her up to her magnificence and distinctiveness. This inner knowledge, placed within her by the Universal Feminine Consciousness, is not found in the superficiality of life. But once disclosed to the searcher this wisdom inspires the female to nurture herself back to self-empowerment. By reconnecting to Cosmic feminine intelligence she can retrieve her authenticity, the true self that she is losing sight of. It is the path all women must return to *NOW*.

Embracing her cosmic composition is to liberate herself on all levels of her being. Chart A, in this book, reminds woman as to important qualities associated with her deepest identity. In that identity lies her greater purpose, individually and collectively.

The messages imparted in the following pages are about revering the unique properties found in the female, representative of the macrocosmic SHE. The universal feminine force is comprised of a wealth of properties, most as of yet unknown to humankind. However, select ones are obvious in the design and attitudes of earth woman as we investigate their purpose here.

Living true to the real self is every woman's birthright; it is her **immediate** destiny. Women have gradually surrendered this right by allowing themselves to be minimized over thousands of years. To date, the female remains entrapped in cultural and religious beliefs that have been adapted to serve the needs of the male ego. It is difficult to break apart these deeply rooted traditions when woman is unsure as to how to proceed. As a result, submission and quiet desperation often result from inaction.

The Woman's Way, which I keep referring to in this book, is really about living through right brain intelligence. Right brain properties emphasize feminine traits while male traits originate from the left brain. Yin, or right brain consciousness, exhibits such characteristics as nurturing and emotional sensitivity which are supportive and empathic. Working with abstract thought, it provides for us the traits of creativity, imagination and intuition. Yin is unity minded. It is also concerned with the inner and higher worlds of reality as well as with the past and the future. Liberal and flexible in problem solving, it is also wisdom oriented and spiritually inclined, embracing unproven truths from an inner sense of knowing. These are but a few of its intelligences.

The Male's Way or Yang left brain consciousness exhibits properties that rely upon logic and reason. Thoughts are concrete, based on facts and practicality which are rational. It is detached rather than unity minded. The left brain is the home of the ego-self or me-consciousness and is concerned with only the physical, outer reality and the present. Being conservative and structured, it relies exclusively on academic intellect, especially math and the sciences. It can therefore only comprehend through proofs (facts) and their conclusions.

The two are very different yet complement each other. Both have valid contributions to offer in this unique state of separate inter-beingness. This duality is set up, through universal programming, to work in a state of balance to provide whole knowledge for us to learn from. These two differing halves are a representation manifest of two greater dualities of universal intelligence referred to as the cosmic feminine and masculine principles or universal positive and negative charge. Cosmic duality has long ago been proven (since light separated from darkness) and re-creates itself constantly to this theme. It expresses itself not only as the left and right brain, or the male and female, but continues all the way down to the minutest representations of the atom molecule with its positively charged proton and its negatively charged electron. The state of separate inter-beingness of dualities working together in harmonious co-existence is the Universal Law of Balance. This particular law, applying to all that is, is not being respected by humanity and as we defy it we suffer and create destruction.

By continually ignoring the right brain's reservoir of unique intelligence, by repressing the ways of the woman in a male egocentric world, we limit our knowledge. Right brain thinking provides humanity with different insights, the woman's ways of looking at life's challenges, offering other perspectives and solutions to our woes. Humanity appears to be half-witted as it has become primarily left-brain dependent, working with but half of a whole, much like standing on one leg.

Chart A lists important properties of a woman's COSMIC BLUEPRINT. This chart re-introduces the reader to that place where she can find her deeper identity and return to being true to herself. Lost woman, no longer attuned to her inherent nature, needs to re-discover herself. Numerous books about the properties of the Feminine have been written in the last fifteen years, it is definitely not a new topic. What is new is the message of urgency interwoven into this book. These earlier books about who woman really is have prepared her for this time. Now she must transform this knowledge into action, for collective women's energy is the next awaited savior to rescue humanity, which is destroying everything in its path including itself. Without a doubt, it is crucial to bring forth these core properties that represent Goddess intelligence.

The scream for equality, as in feminist movements, has some purpose. In my view it is less effective than the demonstration of unshakable self-empowerment coming from women who really know who they are, women living as per their blueprint. This is wholeness of being.

Men in Western cultures are now beginning to cross the

threshold into the woman's world as some become stay-at-home dads or pursue careers more suited for the woman's energy. The female, on the other hand, is moving into jobs that have been primarily occupied by the male.

Even as both genders are now more willing to exchange roles, and rigid and social stereotyping softens, this does not imply that one should be morphing into the other. No matter the pressures of outer circumstances, women as well as men must remain faithful to their cosmic blueprints. We are an active extension of polarities created by cosmic programming that is unchangeable. The uniqueness of the female and the male create the special whole called humanity. Within that whole lies all its future possibilities as two polarities, or two halves, contribute *equally* their differing properties. It is definitely the time for these two sides to become unified with the one purpose of re-attuning humanity through this union of earthly and celestial forces.

Preserving balance in dualities is what the workings of the Cosmos is based upon. It is the dynamic interplay of these opposites, mutually attracted to one another, that gives rise to continual movement, expansion in our universe, creation and evolution. We, therefore, start to realize that if all dualities are meant to contribute equally, male and female energies are no exception if humanity is to thrive. Women who remain invisible and powerless in a man's world need to realize this fact.

They need to look beyond the stars and embrace higher truths with their governing laws. In so doing, they will realize that they too are sovereign beings. No longer will they accept abasement by kneeling at the foot of a king's throne. They will do what rightfully needs to be done. They will assume the throne of the Goddess-Queen. It is only by being aligned with the Law of Universal Balance that the masculine and feminine energies can hope to co-create, side by side, a wholesome humanity.

At the beginning of this book, to lay the groundwork, a handful of historical facts have been resurrected to remind us of some of the circumstances that led to a precarious imbalance between male and female energies. This information is meant to entice lost woman to recommence investigation of her true makeup by reacquainting herself with some of the properties of the Universal Feminine as listed in Chart A of this book. Everything is a process. Woman first needs to KNOW HER REAL SELF. As a result of this knowledge she liberates herself and is then in position to propel her identity into the world as representative incarnate of the Divine Feminine. Full expression of the self is her freedom, as it is intended to be. We need urgently to return to feminine values to halt humanity's rapid degeneration and to clean up our polluted consciousness and toxic environment. Right brain thinking focuses upon such things as a strong sense of community, nurturance and compassion, revering family and its values, developing empathy, relying upon intuition, developing our creativity, returning to nature and focusing more upon spiritual centering which supports interconnectedness.

The following quote by the late Mary Wollstonecraft, a British author on women, contributes to the message of this book nicely:

"I do not wish women to have power over men, but themselves."

# SECTION 1

# 1

# The Millennium of the Great Mother

It is impossible to pinpoint the exact moment of a new beginning. One just senses a shift of sorts as it gains momentum and begins to unfold. An intent of this book is to provide one way to lead women to the gateway of their future.

As the sun sets on a world saturated in patriarchal dominance, there is magic in the dusk. The earth eases once again into darkness, a stillness that appears empty. Yet, it is a night pregnant with potential. Luna, in her fullness, boasts her splendor. It is now that she reveals her true self in her eerie light of moonbeams. Of course, this deeper nature has always been there dancing in the shadows.

This night she unveils herself as Diana the moon Goddess, one representation of the Divine She. Some call her the moon queen. This night she is not but an object in the sky, rather an undeniable presence calling out to every woman on behalf of the universal feminine consciousness.

For it is time for change through revelation.

The Divine Mother, or cosmic feminine, wears many faces. Historical accounts, allegories and myths keep her alive even in this, a man's world. Become aware that her energy is about to be transformed into determined purpose as She ignites the flame of the feminine principle in all women, Her spiritual warriors: swiftly, as one lights every candle on a birthday cake; methodically until each has been awakened by the flame. With this gesture, She imprints her message within the female:

"The age of the Feminine Divine has returned. As her energy courses through you, fill every corner of the world with the ways of the woman. For the sake of an ailing planet, and an ailing humanity, rediscover ancient truths." Tomorrow is upon us. As cosmic winds begin to stir her spirit women are called upon to act.

We must usher in the new dawn by honoring woman's inner wisdom, also known as the eternal light of Goddess intelligence. We need to connect to Her essence soon. We must also become very vocal in representing and protecting Mother Earth, for woman is an extension of Her as well.

# 2

# Gnothi Seauton or Know Thyself

Woman, one of the marvelous creations of universal intelligence. When in her element, living true to her nature, she is empathic, intuitive, soulful, compassionate and devoted to the ways of the heart. These qualities are but some gifts she shares, connecting and contributing to life from a profound place. She offers a sense of depth that balances the shallowness associated with life lived in a superficial way.

She can acutely sense what is needed from the standpoint of love. From this point she continually pacifies and transforms. This is one of her magical powers, and every woman has it, for just as she creates life in the womb she also sustains all life as her nurturing abilities nourish humanity. This is her deeper calling, her greater purpose in the universal plan. Wherever she lives on the planet, whatever she chooses to do or become, it is her destiny to lead with the heart. This is the woman's way.

In today's developed countries, especially on the North American continent, the female is falling from her own grace because she is losing sight of her complete womanness and with it her personal power. She has become incomplete or lost woman by either repressing part of her feminine force or by developing male characteristics to survive in a male dominated world.

We think we know who we are, yet it is only in a superficial way. Our deeper identity is as threatened as is Mother Earth herself at this time, both due to neglect.

To know the core self and then to express in totality that self was a journey taken by women in past civilizations as a passage towards self-realization. Through rituals and instruction wise women circles passed down their knowledge of what a woman really was. Sadly, today, entangled in hectic lifestyles that overwhelm and with the disappearance of women's circles, women are getting further and further away from their inner truth or real identities. Being caught up in the throes of modern ways offers them little time or opportunity to journey the journey that leads back to who they really are.

Now, more than ever, this must change for humankind is in peril of complete disintegration as a lopsided humanity, ruled exclusively by one-sided male views, continues to dominate the world. A woman has no choice but to rebalance this unnatural condition by reclaiming her *true* self, releasing the benevolent powers associated with her passive warrior side. These powers are based upon unwavering truths of the heart and her sense of connectedness that unifies. She is deemed a passive warrior yet is bold in spirit and influential. Her innate wisdom, such as the knowledge that love prevails, heals, enriches and gradually transforms is a part of her heartfelt ways that can veer a terminally ill humanity in the direction of rebirth.

It is women's turn now, for the greater good, to become the phoenixes that rise from the ashes of inferiority and validate themselves by heeding the call of the Feminine Consciousness. Not as ball-busting amazons, dominance-seeking women or resentful feminists, but simply as individual and collective women armed with confidence in their unique magnificence. A part of which is their natural ability to think with the heart. In that way of living women can move to the front lines to effect global change. In so doing women in action become love in action, which is a needed solution for a world that has devolved into beings of hate, greed, violence and self-centeredness.

After an explanation of charts A and B found in the back of this book it will become clearer as to why the burden of change rests upon the shoulders of the feminine gender. There is a certain type of energetic force now needed to incite movement in a different direction while raising consciousness at the same time. That energetic composition belongs to the feminine principle that at this stage of our evolution only fully manifests itself in females. It is as powerful a creator as is the energetic composition of the male principle, but in an entirely different way.

Yet, it has been suppressed, raped, silenced, humiliated, disrespected, attacked, hated, misunderstood, abused and brainwashed throughout the ages. Yin energy is continually being trampled upon by its partner in duality, the yang energy. To no avail, for within the woman the indestructible Divine Feminine lives on. She is not in a weakened state or convalescing; She is simply waiting for that right moment to balance a universal imbalance that threatens the survival of an entire planet.

We must help initiate this movement by once again remembering what the cosmic feminine represents in our womanhood, and return to the ways of the woman. As we re-visit the properties of the Feminine Divine we need to reclaim Her WITHOUT FURTHER DELAY for humankind is in distress. This is the real purpose of this book. Woman can start by taking the Greek words of wisdom *Gnothi Seauton* or "know thyself" more seriously.

# 3

# A Wee Bit of History

Feminine, cosmic energy coursing through the universe and throughout every woman, is the Goddess of one thousand names: Divine Mother, Great Mother, archetypal feminine, MA, MA'AT, Feminine Divine, Feminine Principle, Cosmic Mother, Sacred Feminine, Sophia and Yin are but a few of its titles. They are derived from mythologies of various countries, from paganism and from esoteric (timeless, hidden) sacred wisdoms also known as cosmic truths. They are names that were comfortably used before the advent of Judeo-Christianity and other male-based religions that supported a patriarchal way of life, annihilating the feminine consciousness and her ways.

Humanity's history of just the last seven thousand years alone overflows with information pertaining to oppression and injustices against women. As male-run societies became a way of life, females were relegated to servitude as well as to child bearer. They have always been labeled as the weaker sex, not only physically but as per their level of intelligence and competence. The oppression of women worldwide stems from the male's core makeup, or cosmic blueprint, which is found at the end of this book. His innate nature makes him aggressive, driven towards control and domination. The thirst for this type of power has led men to continually war amongst themselves. It has escalated over the ages to worldwide violence; included in that is the inhumane brutality and disfigurement of women. The major religions, Judaism, Christianity and Islam, worship only a male supreme being and fuel the fires that have led to actual hatred of women. Through twisted dogmas, women are still labeled as impure, sin-ridden, sexually evil, second-class humans or worse still, subhuman life forms.

There was a time in old Europe when the feminine consciousness was respected. Joseph Campbell, a well-known American mythologist and writer, referred to this period as the Age of Harmony, historically known as the Paleolithic era. Commencing in 25,000 B.C., it lasted until 5,000 B.C. During this time frame, nature-based spirituality or nature mysticism was practiced by pagans. *Paganism* simply means *by country people* from the Latin word *"pageni."*

Under the influence of woman's ways, people had an intimate relationship with Earth. The land was deemed sacred; its destruction and that of its creatures was unheard of. These ancients recognized that the planet was a living consciousness providing selflessly for Her children (much like any good mother would do). The Great Mother was alive in them by their deep connection to Her through rituals.

These rituals were offerings of animals, food, herbs, pottery and the like. Through these beliefs, the Cosmic Feminine, represented partly in the powers of nature, flourished. Around 5,000 B.C., there was a radical shift in old Europe. Male nomadic tribes began invading the country. The age of the (male) aggressive warrior extinguished the age of passive Goddess consciousness.

Later, with the onset of the Christian and Muslim religions, the woman's way was further curtailed. Why, because everyone is aware these two great influences are patriarchal. Messages in each became distorted in favor of dominion of men over women and all living things (including the planet). With a monotheistic male God, the onset of abasement of women as worthless, and spiritual leadership by men only; male egos fed off this and fattened.

Interestingly enough, these two religions, as well as Judaism, have the same family origin. Their founding father was Abraham, yet they war amongst themselves to this very day. History overflows with men initiating wars; men, *not* women. For *true* women, as passive warriors, do not entertain these thoughts.

Love, not controlling power, peaceful method not aggression, are the driving forces deep within this type of authentic female who fully expresses her cosmic blueprint.

These three major faiths helped birth fear, violence, and superiority attitudes. This is not the intended spiritual way of a peaceful deity, nor is it woman's way. That leaves it as being man's way. I am not implying that men are bad and only women are good. I am simply pointing out that anything left unchecked, in this case the male ego run amuck, can in its excessiveness cause the imbalance and destructiveness we see running rampant today.

Being its polar opposite, the feminine Yin is the only energy that can balance Yang, as per universal patterns of behavior of polarity that continually endeavor to recreate harmonious balance from chaos. Looking at global disquietude, we can actually feel worldwide instability creating mounting inner and outer tensions. Simple common sense dictates that this state is unnatural and goes against our innate nature programmed for mutually beneficial co-existence. Women, as peaceful warriors or beings of the heart, must become the new leaders that will take us back to homeostasis, dissolving chaos and insecurity caused by such things as heartlessness. Even the relatively new Bahai faith of the Middle East, with its millions of followers worldwide, supports gender equality as the way of tomorrow. It claims that a new civilization will be formed in which female qualities such as tender heartedness will rise and balance masculine dominant insensitivity and indifference.

Historical events such as male God monotheism and the destruction of the feminine way helped to disconnect us from the Earth Mother, the ways of the peaceful woman, from the classic Goddesses that helped define her and from unity mindedness. Though subdued, the doctrines of the Feminine Divine continue to persevere today as hidden knowledge waiting to be redis-covered. As mentioned earlier, many books have been written on this topic to keep Her in plain view. In the 1970s when the Gaia hypothesis claiming that the planet was a living, breathing organism, resurrected itself, Mother Earth, now with a recognized consciousness, fed the resurgence of Divine Feminine energy. Woman is the holder of the secrets associated with nature, as one aspect of her inner identity.

Earth is one feminine representation of what some refer to as God force or more appropriately, androgynous, universal intelligence. The feminine is not inferior nor can the balance between her and her masculine pole ever be compromised.

I quote Genesis 1:27: "God created mankind in His own image. Male and female he created them."

Ancient or esoteric wisdoms know this as a truth, one of many composing universal laws. Even Western modernism with its patriarchal tendencies cannot alter the unchangeable reality of the universal way of balanced duality. Neither can Islamic laws that state that woman is worth but one half of man. Yet, these very laws are based upon Muhammad's teachings that state that "Women are the twin halves of men" and "The rights of women are sacred. See that women are maintained with full rights granted to them." How did these and other such quotes from this prophet become so distorted that Muslim women today have been degraded into being worth half of men? Yet, the esoteric wisdoms of ancient Sufism based also upon the teachings of Muhammad recognize the equality between genders. There is no shortage of brainwashing messages found in male created religions such as in this Orthodox Jewish prayer: "Blessed art thou O Lord our God and King of the Universe that Thou didst not create me a woman."

The two poles of feminine and masculine are also called by many different names such as yin and yang or the negative and positive. These poles are meant to unite harmoniously without friction. One part of a polarity cannot dominate the other without eventual chaos, as is the case in today's world. Cosmic duality originates from one primordial energy that all is created from.

"When you make the two one, when you also make the outside like the inside; when you make the female and male as one, then you will know the peaceful kingdom of God" (Gospel of Thomas).

Peaceful simply means *in a state of harmony*. Hinduism supports this by its writings in the Upanishads that state "Perfect halves that make the perfect whole" when referring to the natural coming together of man and woman.

Unity mindedness is the foundation for the new world order. That means, amongst other things, male and female unified, not as one but as equal halves sustaining the whole it creates which is called humanity.

Primordial consciousness has provided coding in all our cells to show that God/Goddess co-exist in all things equally. In humans we experience it through the union of the egg and sperm.

Yet, the overly empowered male ego in its arrogance or ignorance has come to defy any universal truth that will undermine its superiority. One way is male's insistence on minimizing the importance of yin by repressing her and maximizing the properties of yang. He, himself, can never be a complete reality in itself by dominating his polar opposite. He has to finally accept that he is but one half of a reality, equal not superior. If you think that the male dominance problem in an advanced society such as North America is practically non-existent, think again. Subtle examples are everywhere. Just take the cartoon mascots found on the front of cereal boxes that all children stare at every morning as they eat. Ninety five percent of these role models for kids are male, such as; Tony the Tiger, Toucan Sam, Honey Comb Bear, Captain Crunch, Lucky the Leprechaun, Frankenberry, the list is extensive.

Further to this, my niece told me a story that supports the ongoing abasement of women. At a world renowned Canadian university her friend recently requested an interview for acceptance providing a glowing resume of marks to be admitted into the medicine program. When no one even acknowledged it she insisted on a meeting with the Dean of the university. After looking over her application he admitted to her that it was definitely worthy of consideration and the only reason it may have been by-passed was because she was not a male!

Today we are struggling with the unnatural, chaotic world we have created due to this unstable imbalance and it is frightening that it is still a way of life. Men's cultures influenced by religious or philosophical thought have developed strong features that exhibit dominating, patriarchal views. For example, Confucianism insists that wives obey their husbands without question. Until recently, Jewish tradition permitted only male rabbis. These types of distorted thoughts and actions are on the surface only. As we delve into hidden truths, ancient mystical traditions and esoteric wisdoms, we are instantly exposed to the real governing truths of universal laws that attempt to right our ignorant wrongs. Adjusting imbalance by moving towards a higher consciousness or more expansive knowledge is the resolution for a decaying humanity and, as a direct result, a now decaying planet.

Marija Gumbutas, renowned archaeologist and author, has devoted her life to studying the ancient civilization of old Europe before the shift of 5,000 B.C. According to her findings, the age of the Goddess was definitely a way of life between 25,000 B.C. and 5,000 B.C. The eldest woman of each clan was the revered priestess or wise woman. She knew the secrets of nature's cycles, about planting, harvesting, gathering and preserving. She had extensive knowledge as an herbalist and healer. She was also the primary caretaker and nurturer. Her innate wisdom coupled with her life knowledge made her the hub and strength of her clan.

As of 5,000 B.C. there were male nomadic invasions sweeping parts of the European continent and over time the temples of the

Feminine Divine were all destroyed. The fertile Goddess statues were replaced by male God statues, such as Zeus, Hades and Apollo. Women lost all power and became male possessions. This trend continued when male dominant churches started having power over the people, falsely implying that these types of women, who secretly still followed ancient ways of the Goddess, were witches and started to eliminate them from society.

The ancient mysteries of the Earth Goddess, a natural part of women, was simply not understood by the male and that which is not understood is feared. She, and all the women that associated with Her, had no recognition in a world that was forcefully and brutally shifting into patriarchal consciousness. Yet, thousands of years later, women are beginning to climb back up the mountain they were all thrown down from. Their intent is not to topple the male, but to take their rightful place next to him.

Intuitively, and at times unconsciously, women are on the move upwards. Even though they might not be aware as to the deepest reason for this collective movement, it is apparent as to why to those who study the esoteric truths of universal balance.

It is timely for many reasons. Urban women have for the most part forgotten the dance of natural woman to the harmonies of nature. Out of necessity to preserve Earth as well as protect organic farming, they will again take steps to remember. This forgetfulness in women is partly the cause of Gaia's great distress, and as a result She is initiating women's reconnection to Her.

As well, it is woman's spiritual tendencies and nurturing abilities that must now surge to the fore to halt the epidemic of fear and violence due to the male's aggressiveness and insensitivity. Even though deep within our being we know that acts of killing and violence are acts against conscience, societies are exhibiting the alarming attitude of detachment that is so much a property of male, left brain thinking patterns. It is only in the resurrection of the powers of womanity and the application of her caring ways and sensitivity that Mother Earth and the human family can rebalance and heal.

As women gain awareness as to their programmed roles in humanity they can choose to become a part of the solution. Women can proceed to release themselves from states of submission, acceptance and fear that paralyze them and the progress of the race. Since the peaceful Paleolithic period women have been abased. The gradual stripping of her power has lasted for 7,000 years.

The inquisitions of Europe, commencing in the late 1100s and lasting seven centuries, claimed the lives of entire groups, as well as individuals labeled heretics of the church's dogma. Included in this dark period were a hundred thousand or more females following the women's way who did not conform, being of an independent nature. The witch hunts dating from 1350 until the early 1600s made up the most intense period. The Church, referring to these women of the earth as satanic servants, instilled fear in the masses. Brainwashed, they supported the Church's wrongful accusations and actions. It became a premeditated holocaust of women, and did an effective job of destroying the Earth Goddess culture.

The rape of women's core identities has escalated into the rape of the ultimate feminine entity. From those beginnings to now, the Earth has quietly suffered her despair through industrial, capitalist and technological ages as she continues to be ruthlessly victimized. When will this end? When will the male's insatiable desires for self-gratification stop overriding his conscience? Having dominion over nature simply means being caretakers and protectors of it.

It is obvious that for thousands of years the wheel has been turning downward for the feminine consciousness. Why, one asks? How could this have happened? One good reason is that woman is non-aggressive by nature, being the polar opposite of the male. Her passive resistance was no match for the onslaught that caught her rather unprepared by nomadic invasions and, later on, male preferring religions. Perhaps, if women could have worked collectively, the outcome might have been different. But technology was non-existent and it was hard to rally in force when one had no way of communicating with other women in scattered villages.

Today, of course, it is so easy. Even if we cannot come together in body we can support each other through spirit. Advanced methods of communication have made that possible! Your presence and encouragement can be sent and felt anywhere around the world at a moment's notice.

So as women struggled, often alone or in small groups, their power was limited. Further disintegration of the feminine way ensued with the advent of Judaism and Christianity. The establishment of monotheistic Judaism resulted in the complete displacement of Goddesses in favor of the male God Yahweh. Later on, to abet the trend towards unchallenged patriarchy, the Christian Church in cahoots with the male governing Roman Empire, established with ease its male God dogma. This encouraged the distorted belief that the male air of superiority was Divine Will, easing many a male's conscience, I am sure.

The Church influenced the masses in supporting Roman heads of State while the Roman government handsomely fed the church coffers. Constantine strengthened the ties by becoming the first Roman Emperor to defend and encourage the Christian way, creating the Romanized Church, today called the Roman Catholic Church.

At this stage in history let us pause and look at the position of women. God was now a male deity, governing heads of the rapidly expanding Roman Empire were all male and only men could be dignitaries of the Church. If this were not enough, priests were forbidden to marry for fear that the evil ways of women would corrupt them. Even today, the Roman Catholic Church does not recognize married clergy or women of the cloth but homosexual priests are welcome in the fold. As well, until 200 years ago, the Church was involved in social debates which questioned if women even had souls! The Pandora box of sins of the male clergy worldwide, now being exposed, are swept under the carpet of the Vatican. Can male dominance and its arrogance be any more glaringly obvious?

Ironically, while religions have gotten away with abasing women, they proudly display the symbols of the cross in its various representations. Whether it is the Christian crosses, the Egyptian ankh, or the Celtic cross, they are all esoteric symbols that represent the perfect union of earthly forces (yang) with celestial forces (yin)!

Until recently, male-based religions, influencing many cultures, have remained unchallenged by womanity due to their fear. But times are now a changing after a long winter of feminine discontent. Even as I write this, it is evident that one major influence, Christianity, is losing ground with its once devout followers, as churches become emptier. Although the teachings are still of tremendous value, it is none the less becoming dissatisfying to embrace a set dogma that is not progressive and unable to provide the answers that would bring peace to a violent world. This is because the teachings are not only dated but more importantly they are incomplete, especially in the New Testament pertaining to the messages of Christos, Jesus. Hundreds of years after this wise man lived, the foundational scriptures were altered. Some were modified, others were excluded as the Bible was being written by male only dignitaries of the Romanized Church.

Christ's teachings (Christos means teacher in Greek) came from esoteric knowledge, cosmic wisdom that the masses would never be able to comprehend or access. For example, His knowledge pertaining to the balancing of universal polarities to initiate harmonious co-existence was simplified and taught as equality between male and female. In this way the female energy would no longer be stifled and would be at par with male energy. However, hundreds of years later, as the writings were being assimilated by councils of holy men, they were lacking Christ's depth of wisdom and they were unable to see the bigger picture, the universal truths that we are supposed to align with.

All they were aware of in their limited views was that these new teachings did not entirely support the rabbinic laws that their way of life was built upon. These laws had been intact for thousands of years. The Prophet's words threatened these laws when He began promoting equality between men and women. So they opposed it, not entirely, just by somewhat altering the contents of the scriptures.

In his lifetime, the Christos set examples by treating all women with respect. He repeatedly instructed husbands to be loving towards their wives. Of course, as with all new concepts when first introduced, there is great resistance to change. The semi-altered truths included in the Bible went as far as allowing for women's rights to improve somewhat, but were still laced with messages of their inferiority.

Through tampering, half-truths were created that form some of the teachings of the Bible. Have they been successful in fooling the people? Temporarily, perhaps. As patriarchal dominance keeps weakening the planet and the social fabric that holds humanity together, people are searching for answers, looking deeper for more complete truths. As the cosmic wheel keeps moving, there are finally the beginnings of a downturn for male dominance. The reign of male energy will soon be history. As he slips off the throne, the Goddess consciousness prepares to rise to the occasion, for the simple sake of reinstating equilibrium as per the patterns of the Cosmic Law of Balance.

For higher laws, which we are all subject to, focus impartially upon the continuous creation of homeostasis. Imbalance creates disharmony which in turn creates chaos. If chaos is allowed to prevail, it destroys all in its path. Hence, the masculine/feminine imbalance needs to be recognized as a primary reason for the deterioration of humanity and Mother Earth. Our intelligence is evolved enough now as a race to be able to see and understand the bigger picture.

In the words of *Henry Miller*, author:

"The world is not to be put in order by us, the universe is order incarnate. It is for us to harmonize with this order."

Somehow, opposite energies such as yin and yang help regulate the cosmos and promote evolution. This cosmic reality was first recognized by the ancient Chinese and called by them the Logical Theory of Opposites. In Chinese dualistic cosmology, yin is the feminine principle, soft, cool and passive energy, yang is the male, hard, hot and active energy. As previously mentioned, men and women are simply physical and energetic representations of these cosmic, polar opposites. Balancing these energies in humanity is still very much a work in progress, for males and females are still struggling to find that state of homeostasis that mutually supports and enhances, as it is intended to be. Dualities have always existed in the cosmos. When evolved their differing halves co-exist in a compatible state of separate inter-beingness. So it is destined to become that way, as well, on this planet once the feminine principle is elevated.

"For as it is above it must also be below."

The secrets of esotericism or the greater mysteries remain reserved at this moment, for enlightened masters and teachers who deliver it to us in tiny doses by diluting them into the lesser mysteries. In these simpler forms the unevolved minds of humankind can grasp the essence of the teachings and expand their individual consciousness. For example, in the lesser mysteries the reality of cosmic duality is introduced simply as equality between sexes. The state of "Oneness" is taught as unity mindedness. These lesser mysteries are available to the masses in the teachings of religions. They are also found throughout powerful philosophies such as Daoism, Confucianism, Buddhism, Jainism and Hinduism as well as in nature spirituality that teaches us about the workings of the cosmos by observing Mother Earth.

It is through the cumulative study of these lesser mysteries, that have been revealed gradually over the ages, that we set our foundation and prepare to progress unknowingly towards deeper esoteric wisdom that connects us to understanding and becoming one with the universal laws that organize the cosmos. In a way one might say that this progression to higher understanding is the merging of the two crucial forces of spirituality and science.

As Galileo's colleague worded it, "One tells us how to go to heaven, the other tells us how the heavens go."

It is the combined knowledge of the right and left brain. Together, these teachings provide us with opportunities to develop an expansive comprehension to glean from, directing us towards becoming a stable and harmonious human race.

To become wise is our ultimate destination and it is not about becoming merely an academician. Greater wisdom comes from many sources including an inner sense of knowing. "I just know, for it feels right" is but one example of this occasional connection to that vast knowledge that lies within us. Choosing to investigate the various schools of spiritual thought, or lesser mysteries, is a leap towards enlightenment. At the same time, limiting ourselves by settling for, or preferring only one form, leaves us with stunted wisdom. Choosing none of the available teachings leaves us ignorant.

Summed up, this truth is provided to us in an old Persian proverb:

"One who knows not that he knows not is a fool, shun him.
One who knows that he knows not is a child, teach him.

One who knows not that he knows is asleep, awaken him.
One who knows that he knows is a wise one, follow him."

# 4

# Cosmic Duality

Not to appear to be condescending but if the truth be known, most of us live snugly within the little box known as our lives that serves the self only. Few venture beyond to contemplate the workings of the cosmos. My own insatiable curiosity pushed me out of my box years ago. Hence, I am now one who lives in this world, but am not of it. Manmade restrictive dogmas do not hold me captive, for the most part.

To read on, you too will have to leave the comforts of your box. You will need to become more expansive in thought to investigate deeper aspects of Divine Knowledge pertaining to the Collective Feminine consciousness, which I call "womanity." For those who care to go beyond the information offered in this book, there is a list of suggested readings at the end entitled "Interesting Books" that support the feminine principle and esotericism.

Ancient and current spiritual scholars, as well as sages and prophets, appear to agree upon the following: each of us is a microcosm of the macrocosm known as universal intelligence. At some point we will all have to accept this and realize that Divinity is in our nature. Hence we exist in a duality, an outer and an inner world, a celestial and earthly reality.

Duality governs all worlds and everything in it including ourselves. Opposites constitute the Universe. A polarity consists of two halves with differing properties but are nonetheless inseparable, united by their constant attraction and interaction. On this planet the list is infinite: left/right, up/down, light/dark, wet/dry, optimism/ pessimism, concrete/abstract, solid/gaseous, contraction/expansion, young/old, laugh/cry, spirit/matter and so on. Included in this is man and woman. Duality is not a similar pair, rather a pair of opposites that somehow complement one another with the distinct properties that define each. One duality is not inferior nor superior to the other because one cannot exist without the other. They are interdependent as each property that composes one is simply the extreme opposite of the other's composition. In the example of hot and cold each is unique, yet their properties united represent the WHOLE range of temperature. They rely upon each other to complete one another while retaining their own blueprints.

Another example is the polarity of young and old. Through combining their properties the whole concept of the human's lifespan is created. When we look at color, one pole is white, the other black. In between these extremes is the whole spectrum of color that originates from this duality. Varying halves working in sync help create all the conditions (or states) of the universe.

Going back only 7,000 years, we see how the imbalance between the male and female polarity has escalated. We can no longer deny that humankind, through its nurturance of patriarchy, has severely repressed the energies of its counterpart the feminine. For this has resulted in an ailing humanity, the whole that these two poles are responsible to maintain. It is only through perfect union that we will successfully achieve the oneness with Divine Intelligence that is our programming: in other words, the Divine or perfect state of harmony that results when dualities finally attain equal partnerships. The Law of Cosmic Balance brings polarities together. When these opposites meet and co-exist the outcome is a state of equilibrium or stability instead of chaos. For humankind this is a big part of our evolutionary path. However, by not co-operating with universal intent we are now seriously sabotaging all life on the planet.

It is time now to look at some of the defining cosmic properties of both male and female energies excluding the obvious physical ones. We will be using the two charts at the back of the book to differentiate between these polarities, energetically. As you refer to these charts you will begin to understand the cosmic polarity of woman and man. Finding the inner woman by studying Chart A and living true to that blueprint is what each woman must now fully focus upon. The time is ripe now, we cannot delay any longer. All life on Earth and the planet itself are in great turmoil, in a destructive downspin as we wait upon women to collectively reclaim their sovereignty, wisdom and leadership abilities. This authentic self, or the Goddess within, is what women and civilization have lost sight of. Women must retrieve a part of themselves that is dormant and let it live fully through them and may I say, with full determination now. While aspects of the Divine Her identity are made clear in Chart A, Chart B identifies properties of the Divine He so that woman can see the distinct difference in each.

Having had opportunity in my esoteric research to study different charts that present the opposite (but not opposing) properties of masculine and feminine in its various representations as yin and yang, negative and positive, or anima and animus and so on, I realize the cosmic vastness in it all. Here, these infinite properties have been condensed to the essential expressions of female and male consciousness while in human form.

Take some time now, before we move on, to study these charts and see their differences. It will facilitate understanding the rest of this chapter. As you compare the two defining blueprints of Charts A and B, your first impression may be that male energy appears to be stronger, while female energy implies weakness. This is incorrect as well as impossible.

Presented are simply a list of opposites, as all polar counterparts must be. As mentioned earlier, there is no superiority or inferiority in the universal reality of duality. There is only equality in differentness in order to sustain a particular whole. Each trait of each duality has a valuable function in the greater universal plan. Let us use some properties from the two charts to prove this point:

Is there not as much power in a successful peacemaker as in an aggressive warrior? Is it not true that the trait of flexibility, at times, yields greater results than being too structured? If one is sick we need a healer, not a provider. It serves us better at times to be cautious and conservative, rather than impulsive and risk-taking.

From these few examples alone we begin to see that the woman's way has as much value in maintaining the well-being of society as does the male's way. There is no one right way. Equality is a stranger to friction and dominance.

Using these charts once again, let us look at how the male energy in its exaggeration is now creating an imbalance that is threatening all life on the planet and the natural order of nature, pushing us to the brink of extinction. For while male polarity is still accelerating unchecked into a state of hyper-beingness its counterpart the female polarity is forced to recede into a state of hypo-beingness to compensate.

As it currently stands, saturation by male dominating energy has led to an incomplete or one-sided reality, crippling the progress of the race. Let us now look at some societal imbalances that excessive yang thinking has created.

First, it appears that one's level of intelligence is recognized by the performance of the logical and analytical left brain only. This view is supported in academic education from grades one onward, where math and sciences are now, more than ever, the central focus of education. One cannot go from high school into any creative trade, which is of right brain intelligence, such as culinary school, unless the math is passed. Many right brain dominant, creative students are stifled, unable to pursue their dreams due to their inability to excel in left-brain mathematics and be accepted into further programs after high school. Yet, a science whiz with a strong analytical brain does not suffer any penalty or restrictions from his inability to excel in right brain creative arts. He has no limitations for further education as a result. Extending this left brain preference, it is of no wonder then that scientific and technological research are handsomely funded by male run governments while artistic establishments are underfunded and starve.

Moving on, Yang is aggressive, a warrior and protector by instinct. Violence and war continue to terrorize the world as a result. We remain barbaric. TV shows and movies coming out of Hollywood in the last 20 years and greatly influencing the world are becoming extremely violent without censoring. Ratings show that large amounts of people watch these programs that de-sensitize them more and more. For the most part, gone are the days of feel-good TV shows of the '60s and '70s, they have been greatly minimized.

Male properties focus on physical reality, or the external. Position and wealth support these ideals and materialism is worshipped. The fact that money cannot create a joyful spirit, fill one's heart with love or deep contentment seems of no concern. With this fixation upon the physical, our identities have been externalized. What we have, our status and our looks now define who we are.

Professional sports, business and even our personal lives have become cruelly competitive. This supports the separateness consciousness of the male that focuses upon gratification of the "I" of the lower ego.

We also exploit, without collective conscience, each other and nature. Everyone is moaning about the mounting self-centeredness of others. There is practically no "we" consciousness to be found. Self-centeredness is peaking as more people act without conscience. Society calls them sociopaths and they are popping up everywhere. They no longer are a rarity. They come from the sole attitude of "I want so I will take." Their insensitive, uncaring behavior is based on left-brain me-gratification that does not come from a place of conscience, and so they lie, cheat, steal and murder with no remorse or feeling attached to their actions. There appears to be little moral accountability anymore.

Health issues are dealt almost exclusively with manmade, inorganic pharmaceuticals (a great money generator). These medicines wreak havoc. Inorganic substances are poison to our organic bodies. Side effects of these poisons may well be what we succumb to not our illnesses. Mother nature's cures, the organic alternative, are arrogantly ridiculed. This is because there is no money to be made by corporate giants in herbal cures, natural healing foods, organic spices and teas or homemade mustard poultices. Manmade pharmaceuticals have been proven to kill over and over again, yet they totally monopolize healthcare as the first line of treatment in America to keep fattening corporations that have no conscience but plenty of control over the masses through doctor's persistent suggestions.

Men hold the majority of government positions. This is because North American and European women only earned the right to vote 100 years ago. It is apparent, by the sad state of the world today, that due to the male's self-serving nature, governments do not heed the needs of the people they are supposed to be concerned about.

In the crazed world of material pursuit, stress accelerates and with it comes impatience and inconsideration for others. Indifference (a trait of Chart B) coupled with rudeness have skyrocketed since World War Two. There are even books written about the demise of basic civility. Once again, the lower ego or me-consciousness keeps damaging the universal fabric of inter-connectedness.

Homes, the once flourishing expressions of the ways of the woman, are now empty boxes, as the energy of woman moves into the workplace to seek society's approval and recognition as moneymakers. Being a housewife or homemaker has become frowned upon for there is no dollar worth attached to this type of work. Men are hunters and providers. They consider the home as simply a place to hang their hats. With this male mindset dominating modern societies, women feel further demeaned if they choose to devote their energies to being homemakers creating a welcoming haven for family and friends. When my women clients tell me they are housewives they either feel uncomfortable admitting this or are almost apologetic. Sadly, the victims of this one sided view are the children who become latch-key kids, the demise of family values, the loss of interconnectedness between neighbors and eroded community life.

Aging has become undesirable because it lacks youthful, physical appeal. The elderly are also viewed as being no longer productive. There is no need for them in a fast paced society that is judged by its ongoing achievements and success. On the North American continent, elders are tolerated and placed in trendy, old age homes that isolate and herd them together away from their families. There is no nice way of putting it. In our selfishness and self-absorption we abandon them. Statistics show that there are more people living alone than ever before in Canada and the States. This is hardly a progressive move, since humans are social creatures and can only thrive if they interact and have a sense of belonging. No one wants to feel discarded. Unfortunately, societies controlled by male, left-brain thinking lack sensitivity. Less and less value is placed on the inner wisdom and life expertise attained by elder matriarchs and patriarchs. Instead of connecting to them and gleaning from their accumulated knowledge as younger apprentices, we discard them.

As seen in Chart B, male consciousness is not ecologically minded. They are hardly the stewards and caretakers of the earth. In the last twenty years rampant economic growth and reckless pollution has wrought a devastating toll on the environment. They exploit it without an ounce of remorse and as a result the earth crumbles under our feet and we all swim in toxic soup of our own making. The result is now an angry planet.

In the area of soulfulness and spirituality both are badly neglected. Westernized humanity is busy being impersonal and logical. The domain of higher reality is rarely visited to find the morals or insights offered by inner or higher wisdom.

Finally, death is feared. It is interpreted by left brain thinking as linear, meaning that life has a beginning and a definite end so "live for today and live for your needs" become common attitudes. Since the analytical brain has difficulty in grasping abstract concepts such as the soul's immortality, because everything logically must be finite and fully defined, death is a very uncomfortable and misunderstood subject in Western society.

Now, let us look at the possible contributions of the feminine pole and how it could create a more balanced state on the planet if it would be permitted to fully express itself.

This, according to Chart A, is only some of what she offers humanity.

First, she contributes other sources of knowledge: soul wisdom and creativity. As a part of the unconscious realm, she can easily access them through her intuition or imagination. True woman may be comfortable with left-brain activity, or logic, but her right brain is naturally better developed with its creative and abstract traits. Her influence would encourage an educational system to also focus seriously upon a curriculum that includes a balanced dose of morality, human values, development of unity consciousness, as well as upon one's unique skills, talents and creative abilities. The metaphysical sciences, or spiritual realities, would also be funded by governments realizing the need to develop the inner conscience and higher consciousness. Schools of creative arts would flourish and math and science marks would hold less weight in the final analysis of one's intelligence and potential.

Being more benevolent by nature, women in power would

first look upon peaceful intervention as the acceptable solution to conflict and intolerance.

Female characteristics support inner reality. Living with high ideals of harmlessness and helpfulness would create our primary identity based upon self-worth rather than upon material worth and status.

Through unity mindedness, rather than separateness consciousness, co-operation and consideration would diminish indifference, fierce competitiveness and violence.

By listening to our collective conscience in our daily decisions we would become aware that we are all responsible for the planet's welfare and, in part, the well-being of each other. Selflessness would dilute self-centeredness.

Authentic woman resonates with nature and is a natural healer as a result. If her ways were honored, not ridiculed, natural methods of healing would become a respected complement to westernized, allopathic medicine as it is still in old cultures such as India and the Orient. Organic cures would have their rightful place in modern medicine, primarily focusing upon prevention medicine. By working upon boosting our body's immune response and encouraging its healing abilities, health would become rampant instead of disease!

As individuals that lead with the heart and with a deep sense of interconnectedness, true women in government would tend more to the concerns of the people. Homes, especially those filled with children, would once again resonate with the vibrancy of woman's energy, and neighbors would become more interactive, for women are extremely community minded. A society with a balanced outlook would recognize the importance of her heart energy as invaluable in establishing a state of well-being and cohesiveness within her family. Healthy family units create the foundation that races of people can stably build upon.

Old age, with its accumulated wisdom, would not be overshadowed by the superficiality of youthfulness, for true woman values and nurtures her entire family. Seniors would be revered and included, not neglected and segregated.

Women, as representatives of nature, connected innately to the secrets of Mother Earth, would ensure that the environment is preserved and protected.

Spiritual practices in all forms: contemporary religion, spirituality, ancient nature wisdoms and ageless esoteric truths, would thrive through woman's soulful tendencies.

Finally, death would have a broader perspective. It would not be feared but looked upon as cyclical, a continuum of life with the "self" regenerating indefinitely, as infinite not finite. Thus, we would make greater efforts not to create bad Karma that would follow us to our next destination by acting with greater conscience.

These are but a handful of the obvious imbalances that could be rectified by Yin's unimpeded contributions, greatly improving the current state of the world.

If these two forces had opportunity to work hand-in-hand, each would keep the other in check, not by neutralization, but by normalization.

The matriarchal periods of the past are programmed into our accumulated knowledge as a part of our ongoing development. All this information in our psyches is available to us. In time, we will once again bring this knowledge into the present. All we have to do is choose to remember its value.

When women are true to their nature, they exude ALL the properties listed in Chart A. If they do not remember or abide by their blueprint, they morph into becoming too male-like or become weak representations of female energy. My concern is that I am seeing in modern countries, with a capitalistic focus, more women become too male-like in character as they aggressively compete for financial gain. This is not really their nature and heads in the wrong direction, for it further feeds the current patriarchal mindset and weakens the values of the feminine polarity. This is the lost woman syndrome I speak of. Recently, I read that there is an epidemic of sorts unraveling rooted family traditions in South Korea. In the last thirty years or so, aged parents are being abandoned as their children, ambitious female adults, focus entirely on their careers. There is no longer anyone to care for these elderly and little in the way of social services to step in. This is just another sad example of the value of family no longer being prioritized by woman's ways.

If we look deeper into the hidden mysteries, it is revealed that within every female lies lesser properties of maleness and within man lies lesser properties of female energy; this will be clarified when I speak to you later on about the egg and the sperm as the two foundational energies at conception. This is because we are programmed to evolve into androgynous beings with the union of two separate energies retaining their individual properties. This IS NOT the same as the morphing of one into the other causing loss of core identity. This next step in our evolution can only take place after we have first established beneficial co-existence between the male and the female, each respecting what the other brings to the table. One day androgynous will mean, at only the mental level, the perfect balance of the conscious and unconscious minds, or the full scope of knowledge provided by the intellect and spiritual wisdom. In Chinese medicine, this future of humankind as androgynous is supported by the fact that they have always accepted that the front of the human body resonates yin energy while the back of the body resonates yang and that each organ and gland that is yin energy has within the body its yang partner.

This is our future as we evolve as the microcosmic representation of the macrocosm. First we attain the external balance between male and female which will then propel us towards attaining that perfect balance within ourselves.

Reaching the point of respecting and accepting the supporting differences of both polarities cannot be done through simply studying a book of anatomy and physiology that explains our differences physically and hormonally. It is done through our gift of insatiable curiosity that leads us towards higher knowledge. The last frontier of exploration for humankind will always be the realm of higher truths.

All energies in the universe are programmed to work with their complementing polarity to produce their offspring. Two halves create an extension of themselves or by-product, such as in the positive pollen and negative fruit flower interacting producing fruit.

At this point in time, woman's pressing destiny is to venture towards understanding her core self. In that knowledge, feminine energy will take its place next to man's energy. Once that is attained these two energies can go on to create their by-product, a healthy humanity with its raised consciousness.

The other option is to do nothing, and keep weakening the race. Woman, know your power! The female is often referred to as the celestial womb whereby her energy not only creates from nothingness infinite possibilities, it also transforms chaos into harmony. Chaos is the current state of our world.

All life possesses a common denominator known as energy fields. Males and females are composed of electromagnetic fields that are opposite, yet complementary due to their polarities. Since all life is linked by energy fields, everything is interconnected. It is for this reason that we are interdependent, and contrary, separateness attitudes only weaken this web of life. It is the intellectual, male left brain that is driven by curiosity to understand. It therefore proceeds to separate all things, to analyze, observe and draw its factual conclusions. This is how separateness consciousness escalated in humanity. Isolation is very much a function of left-brain intelligence and has overtaken our lives causing disconnection from one another. The analytical brain is simply not programmed to embrace unity mindedness. It is contrary to the woman's way of right brain dominance. Yet, the two sides are intended to work as a team. God energy and Goddess energy are always entwined and create in that comfortable union *Oneness*. Both are interdependent yet retain fully their identities in the alchemical sacred marriage. There is simply no future in separateness attitudes for it is a half reality. This state is a destructive illusion we keep encouraging as long as women accept Yang perceptions as the only truth and keep themselves inferior.

Hence, humanity struggles. We remove ourselves from the needs of others, isolate ourselves, categorize everyone into groups, decide who is inferior and who is superior, become increasingly insensitive, and try to overtake and dominate one another. This is totally contrary to the state of universal "oneness." Through resistance and ignorance we remain apart from this unifying plan that tries to direct us. As a result we live the consequences of pain, suffering and fear. Yet, through life threatening inconveniences and discomfort, growth will eventually be promoted as we in our weariness start to realize that there must be a better way to live this earthly life. Eventually, our willfulness will surrender to willingness. We will develop in ourselves an aversion to the conduct that creates these overwhelming struggles and make changes or we will go the way of the people of Atlantis.

So one can see that at this time, it is woman that must open herself up to receive and emanate the intentions of the Cosmic Mother, remembering once again who she really is and walking the talk of the basic female properties listed in Chart A. It will only be through her perseverance and insightfulness that change will be initiated.

In time, the equalizing of energies will birth stability out of chaos. Stability brings with it a comforting sense of security. Security creates a sense of calm. Peacefulness is that desired state of harmony that leads to contentment and joyfulness of the race.

Impossible, you say! Idealistic! I can understand the reader's inability to grasp humankind's ultimate destiny patiently waiting at the tip of the horizon. For at this point in our global reality, this appears to be fantasy. Let's take another perspective:

If a child in a third world country has always gone to bed hungry, he knows nothing different. He, therefore, cannot grasp the concept of fullness and contentment. Humanity is that child. Never in the history of humankind have we collectively experienced fulfillment with life and acceptance with everyone. We are all still hungry. Must we hopelessly resign ourselves to this fate or do we have options? I believe that making right choices from our higher conscience is one of the answers.

Another choice, created through awareness, is for women to band together and take hold of the reins of an out of control humanity. Liberating the imprisoned energy of the female principle will direct us towards a new horizon. Sometimes right choices are not appealing because it means expending time and energy to pull us in a new direction so we get discouraged, do nothing and wallow. Stagnation arrests movement and growth resulting in decay and finally death. We can all remain the helpless, hungry child or accept individually who we are, responsible, women adults who must push hard for positive change. There are always reasons as to why not and then there are results. It's always your choice to get caught up in the needs of the self or to work selflessly for the sake of all. Self-change cannot be coerced. We remain free to resist. There is a deep need for change now, movement into a new way of life. Most attuned people feel this. When this urge begins to prompt us individually or collectively we must find the courage to sever the old familiar patterns and embrace the awaiting new ones. All we have to remember is that what we are being directed to is always greater than what we are letting go of. This is evolution.

From the mouths of any learned meta-physicist (spiritual scholar) we hear:

"The goals of universal patterning revolve around the uniting of opposites to work in sync with one another, coming together as needed, moving impersonally towards the greater goal of creating harmony."

This is the human's journey as well. It is only our distorted mindsets of individual separateness that keeps us in a holding pattern that creates fear and pain. This will last as long as we act as if we are apart from the workings of the cosmic plan and one another.

Who then, is the dictator that distorts the mind's perspectives and creates misery and disharmony? It goes by the name of lower ego. Until lower ego is challenged by the soul (higher ego) chaos will continue to weaken humanity. Chart B lists one of the male properties as the lower ego (animal) mind of separateness, while Chart A lists one of the female properties as the higher ego (soul) mind of collectiveness.

Nothing in moderation is destructive. However, too little or too much creates a seesaw effect. Right now, soul consciousness is the kid sitting suspended up in the air with no control, and the big fat kid, or lower ego consciousness, sits on that seesaw at ground level keeping soul force in limbo. The energies of male and female working together is the antidote to the states of hyper-ness and hypo-ness which we have sadly come to accept as normal reality.

Let me give you a great example of feminine and masculine polarities working compatibly in perfect union. Look at the marvel of creation, when resistance is removed and limitless possibilities are allowed to manifest. I speak now of childbirth.

If we, once again, refer to Charts A and B, we observe the following: male energy, representing movement by being a penetrator, unites with the stationary receptacle, which is the feminine energy. The active principle initiates creation with reliance upon the passive principle. The penetrator delivers the sperm to the receptacle housing the egg. Fertilization occurs (or the sacred union of two opposites) resulting in... a creation! If the intent is positive, the physical manifestation of a new whole is not only positive; it is also magnificent beyond our expectations!

Yet, one polarity without the other's full contribution would result in nothing, a void of potential unattained. The secret is working together without resistance or dominance with positive intent to create beauty for the common good. Interestingly enough, in the creation of either a male or female child, both blueprints of this union are coded in the cells, for both the egg and the sperm remain the unshakable foundation that this child was created from, another clue as to our androgynous programming.

The Upanishads, a part of Hindu esoteric wisdoms, plays with the logical brain by explaining how opposites in unity retain their properties at the same time:

"Creation is that which is in motion, yet remains still."

Let us move to another example of two polarities working hand in hand. This next one appeals to the nature woman in all of us. This information was once known to natural woman, but for urbanized woman now disconnected from this aspect of her true self, the following has become foreign knowledge to her. Fruit and nut trees vary in their ability to birth their produce. Some are self-pollinating which means that both male and female flowers grow on each tree. Others, like varieties of apples, pears or the pistachio tree cannot. These female fruit bearing trees need the male counterpart trees to be planted within fifty feet of them to ensure cross-pollination. If not, nothing is created.

The equation of the universe, represented to us over and over again through nature is simple: Two polarities unite, fertilize and through their interaction manifest a whole or wholesome creation for all to benefit from. It remains impersonal, yet consistent without interference from man's self-serving, lower ego, which inhibits only his own progress.

A. The current state of imbalance of excessive (hyper) yang energy and recessive (hypo) yin energy which results in disharmony and chaos.

B. The current state of separateness consciousness

C. A balanced, evolved state of unity mindedness between yin and yang energies

D. The ultimate state of balance and unity that is constantly expressing ongoing harmonious creation.

If one studies the universal yin and yang symbol, we see the concept of two unique energies entwined in physical representation. The symbol is light as well as dark. Yet, each includes an arc cut out of the middle of the other half to symbolize that even though each is separate, it also is a part of the other. As opposites attract, movement is initiated towards union, and towards creation. The male energy as penetrator by itself has no place to create. The female energy offers a receptacle or place that allows for the beginnings of movement to manifest into something. This co-existence and co-operation allows for perpetual motion encouraging change and evolution of new life.

The mystic centers of the yin and yang symbol can be likened to the centre or neutron of an atom. They are both a state of whole beingness and in that harmony do not pull in opposite directions. The center of a neutron is supported by electrons and protons, or positive and negative energy. Yin is a representation of the negative charge, yang is the positive, supporting the mystic centers of the ying and yang symbol.

Now let us jump from smaller examples of duality in co-operation to the grandest planetary example. Mother Earth is the feminine receptacle or womb where life is continually re-created and provides. Nature is our proof. What most of us do not know is that there is an immaculate conception energetically that occurs within the earth each year at the commencement of the winter solstice (Dec. 21$^{st}$). Ancient or esoteric hidden knowledge documents this in different ways. The ray of love, one of seven primary rays, starts to descend towards earth every autumn and recedes back into the cosmos after January 6$^{th}$. As the male penetrator, this energy enters the atmospheric layers of our planet, and eventually Mother Earth herself. By the time the winter solstice has arrived, the ray has penetrated the core of the planet. This cosmic ray, also the provider, has impregnated the planet with the vibrations of unconditional love. All on the planet, with the ability to love, are affected consciously or unconsciously by this surge of harmonic energy. We are lifted into our hearts for a time. One might say it is a birthing of higher consciousness taking place. Love intensifies. The end result is the night of perfect, harmonious resonance known as December 24$^{th}$. Esoterically, it is simply known as the winter solstice period for this re-occurrence does not support or prefer any one religion. This new infusion raises the consciousness of love and humanity evolves a bit more.

The air is thick with a magical peacefulness during this brief time, whether one celebrates Christmas or not. Many stories are told of great spiritual masters symbolically or actually being born during this time period As good-will teachers they are vibrationally compatible with this annual raising of consciousness.

How could this creation of the regular birthing of higher, purer consciousness occur if the dual aspects of the receptacle feminine Earth and the male ray penetrator did not co-operate in this yearly, cosmic spiritualization?

This ray of love and wisdom, providing the connection to the higher realm, emanates also through many world teachers that have continued to solidify this connection, long after it has receded back into the cosmos. Some of the more current messengers include Shri-Krishna, Gautama Buddha, Bahaullah, Muhammad, Lao-Tzu, Zoroaster, Confucius, the Bodhisattvas of the Orient, Hermes and, of course, the Christos.

As mentioned at the onset of this chapter, my intent here is to simply push you further out of your box and show you that while our self-imposed, willful ignorance causes us to continually struggle, the greater truth is that the two dualities (man and woman) could easily work with one another promoting harmony simply through respectful acknowledgement of each other's importance. On other planes of cosmic existence, this is continually happening. Removing the manmade barriers of inferiority and superiority creates union, achieving in time completion, or oneness with Divine intelligence as it is intended to be.

# 5

# Male Seers, Planetary Mothers and Lilith

When evolved, male teachers incarnate they bring with them higher knowledge from the spheres. During periods of accelerated evolution of humankind into elevated consciousness, these master seers become present to the masses. They are always here working behind the scenes, but when humanity is ready, they appear and divulge to us that which we are now capable of comprehending.

For example, it would be of no value to try to impart the teachings of grade four multiplication or division to a grade one student. Their mind is not developed enough to grasp it. Try as they might, the concepts are not understood and they go right over their heads and out the window.

So it is with humanity. Generation after generation, we build upon past knowledge and wisdom inherited through natural progression. All that humankind has learned and experienced courses through our bloodlines. Our entire past history lies within us and sets the stage for future learning. Avatars and world messengers have continually, in our history, infused into the world higher teachings. We are not just dumped here to cope the best we can in a disorganized universe. There is, unknown to us, a plan or path of progress directed by universal purpose.

Each profound truth revealed on how to live more harmoniously within self and more selflessly is a powerful revelation. It is not meant to be just an "Oh really, I didn't know that" fleeting awareness. It is for the purpose of opening the mind and quickening the heart, forever to be imprinted for future generations to use.

While there is no shortage of accumulated wisdom from these Masters available today in books, scrolls, tapes, workshops and through spiritual institutions, this knowledge will simply remain in limbo until the individuals who remain asleep awaken and invite this wisdom into their heart self.

All guiding wisdom for our self-improvement, or for the common good, comes from outside sources waiting to be recognized or from urgings deep within our being. The male avatars impregnate knowledge from the outside into the hearts of civilization because they are the penetrators. They work upon the sphere of the conscious or the known.

At the same time, just as these masters are at work, maintaining dualistic balance are the great planetary mothers, quietly, yet powerfully invoking change from the heart mind outwards. They work from the receptacle itself, which in this case is the heart centre of every person. From inside of humankind moving outwards these feminine avatars work in unison with their opposite polarity to create change from their sphere of the unconscious or yet unknown.

They may or may not reside in physical bodies. While male teachers are often more obvious in their presence because they are associated with the physical realm (Chart B), Feminine Divine incarnates are mostly hidden, as they associate with the abstract realm (Chart A) and work through manifesting vibrations of love by triggering humanity's heart selves through energetic suggestion.

Female masters are not to be confused with the hundreds of mythical goddesses found in history. The purpose of allegorical goddesses is as symbology for all women to identify with as reminders as to who they are. All Goddesses are simply archetypal representations of the universal female energy within us.

Some female, spiritual, planetary mothers have made themselves known such as; the Virgin Mary, Mary Magdalene, Mother Teresa, Mary Maxwell of the Bahai Faith, Teresa of Avila, Helena Blavatsky of Theosophy, and the more current Pema Chodren and Mother Meera.

But for the most part the work of the feminine energy is more subtle and therefore less obvious than the vocal teachings of their male counterparts; different energies coming together in a state of inter-beingness to co-create humanity's evolution.

So it is. Without us even knowing, attempts at rebalancing from the cosmic level are happening in a multitude of ways. The advanced female incarnates dedicated to this are in total service to the energies of the Cosmic Mother, thereby ensuring that the feminine ways are continually influencing us.

Even though these discreet female avatars work on a planetary scale, each woman like you and me, can also choose to contribute in a more minuscule yet mighty way towards recreating harmonious co-existence on the planet. One of the ways of woman is through healing by the inoculation of love, another is through her self-empowerment.

For the next page or so, I will share with you a special moment in my life when I had the privilege of being in the presence of one of these great females. I remain in awe of her devotion and tireless work in helping re-stabilize humanity.

It was in December 2008 in Montreal, Canada that I met her. (Sounds like the beginning of a love novel, doesn't it?) I am not at liberty to divulge her name for she discourages self-promotion. Though she remains inconspicuous to the masses, she is still known to those on spiritual quests or on journeys of the soul. She has dedicated her life, since age 16, to service of the race, to help create higher awareness. For this, she does not take money, for it is her soul purpose. She mentions in her books of enlightenment that she is but one of many current manifestations of the Great Mother pouring love into the planet to offset the suffering created by self-centeredness.

Originally from India, she travels non-stop, does not speak to her audiences, yet receives upwards of 500 people at her sittings. Her work in these sittings is to energetically open your heart up to the pure light and love she pours into you. Each person is with her no more than three minutes. She makes no claims, does not advertise herself announcing her arrival and does not own a private jet. Everything about her is simple, low key and humble. Those who need her find her, for it is never by coincidence that we cross paths. Incidentally, she too was born on December 26th alongside other great initiates supposedly born during the holy winter solstice period I spoke of earlier.

To be in the presence of such a dedicated soul, to experience her in her devotional work with her pure intent, stirs even the heart that is closed. If one person can draw so many and infuse love and hope into all these beings, then what would an empowered, collective womanity be capable of?

We, in our limited perception of ourselves, often think, "What can I possibly do that would make a difference?" After seeing this small woman in person I now know my answer. Anything. Everything with right intent makes a difference.

We are not all destined to become avatars with a massive shift in collective consciousness as our life purpose. Yet, we as women are soulful, nurturing and heart inspired. If we enthrone these greatnesses within us and live nobly, our birthright, the power of the feminine will be glorified through each and every one of us!

Women have no choice, it appears, but to now exalt themselves spiritually and ethically out of conscience. Some, in the process, will leave behind great legacies that change the world. These will be massive thumbprints. Little thumbprints are also invaluable for all life on the planet and the Earth itself need woman's help.

Without being an alarmist, I leave you to draw your own conclusions from the following message from a book written by this Mother Avatar. She states that her mission is simple. She is a vessel of outpouring love and enlightenment to those who remain asleep in the darkness of non-awareness.

She goes on to say that the feminine way is through gentleness, yet strong perseverance. This is the approach that the female masters use to raise consciousness and interconnect-edness, but there is more. She goes on to say that after a period of time if the gentle approach does not attain the necessary results due to willfulness (resistance), other measures will follow. Humankind always has a choice. The choice is to resist through selfishness (I will gladly help as long as I am not inconvenienced) or to surrender our conveniences willingly for the good of all.

This teacher mentions that the other approach, being the last choice, is a destructive one. Tough love is also a teaching tool of any good mother. If necessary, shortly there will be great upheavals and crisis on many levels to bring us to our knees to teach reluctantly through pain, the need to raise the consciousness of humanity so all can survive. Again, I remind you that Universal laws are impersonal. "What goes around comes around," is but one of these unchanging laws. The mandate is evolution by the road that leads to higher consciousness.

It appears we are being forewarned. Our selfishness and preoccupation with the little world of the pompous self will be corrected, for we cannot remain separate from the interconnect-edness of universal ways. We won't survive.

But why would a nurturing, loving, passive feminine cosmic energy bring on destruction? It appears to be a contradiction.

Collective humanity and the planet have to be preserved. But at times, something of a bad seed must be destroyed and re-created. If a farmer sees that his crop is damaged or weak and not yielding he will pull out the plants and re-seed. It is simply survival. As well, no loving parent wants to resort to creating pain for their child even when they refuse to listen and co-operate. Eventually harsher action has to be implemented, as with the farmer's way.

So it is with the Great Mother consciousness as she protects her children. She is correcting not punishing, nor maliciously destroying. If her spiritual warriors, all women that are representations of her on the planet do not respond to her calls, she will impersonally, in time do whatever is necessary to create the shift in consciousness to preserve. This is simply a programmed response to correct the wrong of our own self-destructive ways.

Does this, therefore, make her the terrible mother? In man invented myths and allegories some goddesses created are dark, destructive and non-compassionate. The other side of the feminine energy does indeed exist. But it is not evil nor does it derive pleasure in eating little children whole. Her role is to preserve and create. This is universal love in action; gently or through tough love the objectives are reached.

In readings of mythology, allegories, folklore and spiritual scriptures of various religions, this side of the feminine consciousness is feared, for it is generally not understood. To me this sleeping dragon only awakens when absolutely necessary and provoked. It is a last resort and should be in every mother who prefers to teach and encourage through the woman's way, the loving way. Both sides are so innate in us that they are primordial (ageless).

Let us look at one representation of this dark, or shadow side of the feminine according to Jewish folklore. According to these writings, Lilith was the first woman created before Eve and was therefore, the first manifestation of feminine energy onto the planet. Adam was the first male. As the story of co-creation unfolds, feisty Lilith runs away from Adam for she realizes that he does not consider her as an equal. She refuses to be submissive because within her core being she knows the universal truth.

However, she is misinterpreted and made out unfairly to be the terrible feminine, evil, destructive and a troublemaker. Eventually, she is banished into the wilderness, by who is my real question? Is it perhaps by the loving God of compassion and fairness? This doesn't sound quite right. Or perhaps it is by the I'm-so-full-of-myself Adam. Perhaps, it is by the male writers of this tale?

Eve is Adam's second mate. She is more passive, nurturing and gentle, which is simply the representation of the other side of the feminine. Eve is tricked into eating the fruits of the forbidden tree of knowledge and greater truths by guess who? Lilith disguised as a serpent. Adam is persuaded by Eve to munch as well and humanity is then doomed to pay for this.

From this story Lilith appears to be simply horrid for she alone has caused all the pain of humanity. Everyone needs a scapegoat so they can remain irresponsible! The name Lilith brings to mind images of seducer, liar, and manipulator who brings about death and destruction with her ways. She is (intentionally?) misunderstood.

Interestingly enough, what is glossed over if not omitted in this one-sided interpretation of Jewish wisdom is a very important, not to be missed truth of ageless cosmic wisdom that pre-dates Judaism.

True, the snake, a reptile, is cold, mysterious and therefore something to be feared on a physical level. However, in esoteric spirituality, the foundation of all religion, the serpent is revered. For the serpent has always been associated with the deepest truths and is the bringer of enlightenment. It is a blessing to see one in your dreams, for it is a great teacher.

Victorian poet Robert Browning wrote a poem about the actual friendship between Lilith and Eve or the whole of the feminine consciousness coming together. In the poem Lilith claims that she truly does love Adam and therefore wishes him no harm. Adam, in esoteric literature, represents the first race of humankind known as the adamic race. Her intentions are honorable because in her love of humankind, of both Adam and Eve, she is concerned in revealing cosmic truths that would enhance harmonious co-existence.

So does the cosmic feminine consciousness use its powers for evil intent? Of course not, that would be self-serving and self-gratifying. This is not a part of the makeup of higher consciousness that represents itself as the woman's way. This level of consciousness transcends personality and lower ego.

When the female part of the universal principle we define as the Cosmic Mother will wreak havoc to rebalance, don't take it personally. It is simply a part of the natural order of all that is. While you are ducking for cover, take a moment to marvel at the mystery of all love even tough love with its intent to heal and transform.

Since the 1970s and the Gaia hypothesis, there appears to be a re-kindling of woman's type of spiritual practices that many old Eastern philosophies resonate with. We are now incorporating into westernized, male influenced societies such things as: nature worship, organic farming, herbology, aromatherapy, natural medicine, hands on healing, yoga, meditation, visual-ization therapy, esoteric astrology and numerology, workshops on intuition, soul therapies, spiritual women's rituals and the resurgence of Wiccan knowledge. As well, with environmental concerns in the headlines, the push back to the woman's natural ways is gaining momentum.

It is time to return to the true woman beckoning from within us. She is our answer. The ancient Jewish text of the Zohar encourages us to do so with this prediction:

"The light of the moon (the female) will become like the light of the sun (the male)."

If women choose apathy or resistance, then I will leave you with this humorous thought: "If we insist upon remaining bent over with our heads buried in the sand, one thing is for certain...we will keep getting our asses kicked."

Hasn't womanity suffered enough?

6

# The Way I See It

I read an article in the Montreal Gazette that commenced with "What happened to the global economy? All of a sudden all hell is breaking loose!" I could add to that by asking "What has happened to our climate? All of a sudden all hell is breaking loose!" Or how about "Whatever happened to civilian safety and civility on our streets?"

In North America and Europe, financial crisis, environmental upheaval, violence, terrorism and mass killings by distraught everyday people are common day-to-day fare. When a destructive shift finally kicks in it is merciless. Yet, we have had ongoing warning signs regarding the rapid deterioration around us and we just go about our business as if these ominous signs are like annoying flies to be flicked away. Is this happening without our resistance because we are not concerned or choose to remain disconnected to our reality? Is it perhaps due to greediness or stupidity? Are we in denial? Perhaps we are all paralyzed by a state of overwhelming helplessness or hopelessness? Are we learning, against our common sense, to adapt to and tolerate that which is intolerable? I tend to think that it is all of the above.

There is a saying, my favorite one in fact:

"Evil triumphs when good people do nothing."

Maybe it is time for all of us to do something, not just a few of us, for it is obvious that conditions are rapidly worsening. It doesn't have to be this way. I'm not being negative here. It really is worse than it looks! If I was visiting this planet from elsewhere I would high-tail it out of here. Nice place to spend a weekend, but...

I realize that valiant attempts by a few are being made to make positive changes. I applaud them. But a handful cannot possibly do the work of the many. In Switzerland in 2005, one thousand women worldwide were selected to win the Nobel Peace Prize. They were known as the 1,000 Peace Women.

Julia Morton Marr, Canada's peace woman, mentioned then that her concerns were for Mother Earth and felt that we all had to now work together for the environment and for peace.

The important word here is "we" which implies everyone.

World peace and the environment are certainly big topics amongst everyone at this time in our history. From where I see it, a less recognized but serious problem is society's mounting inattention to one another. This "can't be bothered" attitude leads us to become apathetic, indifferent and disinclined to extend ourselves for others, even sometimes our friends. This has nothing to do with anything except increasing coldness of the heart as in inconsideration. This sad reality now surrounds us and penetrates like a chilling breeze, yet we are not yet concerned enough to do anything about it so we uncomfortably adjust. For example, in large cities and their sprawling suburbs people are no longer genuinely nice to one another. This is unacceptable behavior. Sure, people force themselves to be nice with that taped on fake smile. There is also the robotically delivered "Have a nice day" offered by cashiers and servers that really do not care. Let us not forget the insincere "excuse me" as people shove past you and mow you down. Where I live, in the suburbs next to Montreal, people I see all the time out walking but have not formally met look at the ground when passing me rather than just smiling or saying hello! How can we ever hope to become civilized if we are not even civil?

In the meantime, in today's discord more pockets of women need to become involved with the urgent issues of human rights, the decline of family values, animal protection, global poverty, starvation, the rape of the environment, the poisoning of our food, and civilian safety to highlight a few. With so many pressing problems how can we, in good conscience, let others carry this enormous load on our behalf? Our words, concepts and good intentions are cheap, if not followed up by action. We need to overcome, through heightened conscience, our lethargy and excuses. Most of us do not get motivated until our own personal lives are severely affected.

In today's age of literacy, internet and global media, information is readily available. Let us begin, at least, to get informed about the chaos in the world. Then, as women of the heart, let us each act upon this information. Feel into the pain of the planet and its inhabitants. As true woman if you open yourself up and feel from your heart you will sense the desperation around you and will know what to do. Then just do it. Act with the strength and courage of the spiritual warrior that you truly are.

Gandhi once said, "If you educate a man then he is simply educated. However, if you educate woman she educates her whole family."

Women have influence!

To motivate you, here is a sampling of information pertaining to but one area of human suffering that needs our immediate attention, the inferior treatment of women.

One out of three women will become victims of male-based violence. In the United States a woman is beaten every 18 minutes. Five hundred thousand girls under age eighteen are annual victims of white slavery and human trafficking. Millions of women globally are bought and sold yearly as property. Regarding employment in first world countries, it is still commonplace to offer a male, with the same training, a higher salary. In Arab societies I quote directly, "Independent women are subordinates who must be tamed at any cost." The strict Sharia laws of the Muslims promote motherhood, yet deny basic rights to women. It is permissible in some traditions for husbands to stone, beat, sell or kill their wives and daughters especially in Middle Eastern countries. Women in Africa, still under primitive, cultural laws, remain inferior as to their worth. In their culture genital mutilation, as per male insistence, is performed on nearly two million young girls per year often resulting in death. In poorer parts of India women suffer from severe malnutrition for they are only permitted to eat what is left after their men folk are satiated. As well, in India one woman is raped per hour or burnt to death. In China it is still common practice to drown baby girls, abandon them, or place them up for adoption. In Pakistan women are not allowed to own property.

Just these handful of facts support that women still remain suppressed, 7,000 years after the fall of the Matriarchal system in Europe. The laws of the Universal Declaration of Human Rights established in 1948 by the United Nations General Assembly have started to make the corrections necessary. It remains a painfully slow process, unless we all help it along.

The rights of all women are not just about the respect of these laws being initiated, it goes much deeper. Their full liberation extends to honoring their birthright (blueprint) so that each one can intuitively follow and live by the ways of the woman which by definition is her. The ultimate fairness is for her to be able to live freely as per her nature. Since this is not being encouraged, women need to become aware that only in global unison can they initiate these ways that go beyond basic rights. If we leave our power fragmented the whole process will drag its feet. Later on in this book I explain the influence of women's circles that urge us along the path of collective consciousness. For now Charts A and B are invaluable in helping us comprehend the attributes and powers associated with the core identity of woman as well as of man.

# 7

# The Physical, the Unique and the Collective Self

To know oneself completely requires awareness of the three major aspects of the self that define woman. Devoting time to developing and maintaining each is of great importance. The three are our physical self, our soul, and lastly the collective self, which is the state of total oneness with all creation.

Our physicality is often what we get hung up on. We define ourselves through it and spend a great deal of time preening and adorning it. Perhaps that is why we dread dying, because it is the definite end of our physical nature. Even though many do acknowledge the soul self as infinite, it is an abstract concept while the body is a concrete reality. Since the dominating logical brain has great difficulty with abstract reality because it relies upon facts, the idea of a soul self remains uncertain. The fixation remains upon the physical since humanity leans upon left brain thought patterns of yang that supports "seeing is believing."

Everyone that is a student of metaphysical studies or higher wisdoms has come across sayings that state that we are all fools buying into illusions. What appears to be reality to those that are not yet coming from higher consciousness is actually an illusion. In other words, the abstract unseen or inner world is the real thing consisting of the soul and the collective self that endures, while the physical disintegrates over time.

Our physicality is to be honored as the crystal vase that holds the rose of our real being. This vase is fragile and must be well taken care of to ensure its wellness and longevity for it holds our very essence. Its purpose is to keep the real self grounded on the earth plane for a few decades. Our bodies need to remain healthy and be protected from harsh environments, that is all. Way too much time is spent in affluent societies decking out the body like a Christmas tree so it looks nice. More time should be devoted to ensuring that we do not prematurely destroy that delicate vase through gluttony, neglect, laziness, stress and general indifference to its needs.

The second important part of the makeup of a person is their psychological profile and what we do to promote our psychological well-being. In the psyche or soul, we find our positive (not negative) thoughts and emotions, our preferences and dislikes, our morals and values, our unfulfilled passions and hopes, our sensitivity to others, our ability to love unconditionally, our creative expression, our special skills and talents, our developed wisdom to date, and our level of conscience. This part of us is referred to as our uniqueness in the sea of common beingness. Even though we are very much alike, in this area we are individual, for the soul self is the product of ongoing personal development through the ages due to its infinite nature.

Each human evolves by expanding their soul consciousness through life challenges and opportunities, as well as by making efforts to purify any negativity within their thought patterns.

When we are born into our physical nature, our potential for further development begins anew. Once again we are given a span of time to express in our own way our unique gifts and heighten our consciousness. The immortal soul is our suitcase filled with personalized attainments accumulated. We keep building strength of character, morals, virtues, become more loving and develop an array of talents and gifts over many lifetimes as we evolve. In each incarnation we can use everything we have brought with us to further expand our consciousness. We can also choose not to progress much, allowing limiting thought forms to de-rail us. This is also known as succumbing to temptations or challenges set before us to break through.

The first choice rewards us with inner contentment, due to a sense of fulfillment. The other choice leads to eventual feelings of discontentment or unfulfillment with life.

Due to the uniqueness of self on a soul level, no one is vibrationally or physically identical. The pursuit of investigating this part of you is your dedication to self-discovery and is, therefore, a personal journey. Sadly, the majority of people do not ever delve into the originality of their unique selves. Most just gloss over this aspect at best paying little attention to the abstract self. Many do not know any better, while many get caught up in physical reality and are lured into its illusions. Due to this neglect of the inner self, their distinctiveness is never liberated. Not self-realized they die undiscovered to themselves, never acknowledging their soul passions that would have greatly flavored their lives.

Those who take the time to address a nagging inner sense that a part of the self is missing may find answers by visiting a therapist's office looking for direction; direction inward that is. Ironically *psychologist, psychiatrist, psycho-analyst* or *psycho-therapist* are all derived from the word "psyche" or soul. Others may find answers in self-help books, which is the vogue, or they may try to understand the soul through religion.

Moving now into the deepest stratum of our being, we find our common essence at our core. This is the third part of our makeup. The soul self is connected to this. Called collective energy or spirit, it is what feeds vital life force to the soul allowing it to express itself on this plane of existence.

As we know this universal self is our origin. Dualities are its extension of its self and are represented for us here in the polarity of Charts A and B. Vibrationally or energetically at this point in our evolution, humanity emanates primarily either the collective male or female aspects of the universal "one." In other words, The Cosmic Feminine is the energy that is every woman's common foundation. It is this core makeup of woman that has been suppressed by masculine dominant energy on the planet.

The defining attributes of the Feminine Divine are her gifts to every woman. What woman does with these properties is her offering back to the Cosmic Mother. It is also a gift she gives herself. By allowing the feminine principle to be fully alive in her, woman is empowered connecting to her collective identity and purpose. A woman with the above knowledge can easily live in fullness of being by respecting the three aspects of herself mentioned here and in so doing, can easily withstand any assault upon her womanhood. When complete or whole, no one can take her identity away from her.

Secure in this she needs no longer to struggle due to feelings of weakness in a patriarchal society filled with disrespect for her, nor does she have to mutate and adopt manlike mannerisms to gain acceptance. No longer does she need to be submissive or property to be bought, sold, discarded or violated. She needs only to embrace the identities of soul uniqueness and core collectiveness and live in accordance with them.

Womanity remains in a weakened state because she has been forced to lose touch with her common beingness or collective female self, the deepest most solid part of her nature. With eyes to see and ears to hear, I perceive that women have been involuntarily reduced to revealing to the world only the tip of their iceberg. Most of their natural ways have been submerged. Hidden for so long, womanity has now all but forgotten about this submerged part that is the authentic self. The result is that humanity's elusive equilibrium has become even more unstable.

We need to remember that woman is the resonating energy of all that represents earth, hearth and heart consciousness. This is primarily how the Feminine force reveals Herself on the planet. The female aspect of universal omnipresence is prodding us once again. The Goddess is pushing, if not actually shoving us towards remembering her ways. This, in time, will create a surge of Her power that will flow onto the planet and initiate rebalance.

In review, our base is collective energy represented in polarities. Secondly, we are individualized soul energy that is the psyche self, filled with endless possibilities for personal development and unique expression. Thirdly, all this is housed temporarily in a physical vessel. Women need to make a concerted effort to get familiar with their primary base energy that unifies them and humankind. This will diffuse separateness consciousness. If not, we will have to deal with frightening consequences. The soul will lose its earth playground for expression and evolution as humans kill off the planet and terminate the race.

I do not believe that this is the original plan of supreme intelligence but might be the end result due to unrelenting resistance of ignorant people that have been convinced, through lower ego, that they are somehow invincible as a race.

It is only through the consciousness of interconnectedness that is first demonstrated in evolving humans as concern for another, expanding into community mindedness and then finally into awakened global conscience, that the soul self has opportunity to express its loving nature by using its special gifts and skills to augment harmony in the world and selflessly serve.

I feel at this time that the journey back to collective awareness can be more easily done by women forming groups. As bonding is created, sameness on many levels is realized. Once tapped into it collective thought is the uplifting power that overrides separateness consciousness which is always weaker due to its singularity of thought.

The unknowable is a creator. If not, there would be nothing but vastness filled with emptiness. If we are all modeled after this creator, then we too have an ability to create ourselves and our reality. Used in good conscience this is a magnificent gift we have all been given. Used with negative intent or for selfish means it is our individual curse.

In other words, what we make of ourselves and create is mostly a personal choice. Few things are predestined and those that are, are placed in our path to teach us, a little harshly, more about who we really are. Each of us possesses weaknesses and distorted thought forms that if not attended to can impede our growth and produce unneeded suffering for ourselves and others. It is tough life lessons that try to correct this within us. We are encouraged to find our answers by turning to soul wisdom, which is capable of not only finding solutions, but of creating limitless, beautiful possibilities to enhance life. We all have the Midas touch as creators of our own reality. We also have the power to destroy ourselves and take everyone with us.

This fact is written in code in all Divine script.

"Know thyself" and then "become that self" is also about creating the self because we are CREATORS. It is a long and gradual journey to the within, to a deeper reality. The slow process of purification through spiritualization automatically takes place as we journey to the core of our being, to a higher consciousness to meet the other parts of ourselves that complete us. Once again, this is the way of the woman, right brain knowledge that is based on intuitive connection to the unexplainable, undefinable, infinite source that is known by many names.

# 8

# Modern Woman's Inner Whisperings

"Who am I? Why am I? Where am I in life unfolding?"

Perhaps one day, when I am not so busy buzzing around attending to mundane responsibilities and unquenchable desires, I will get around to answering these questions. Someday, when I am so fed up, so weary, so empty or disillusioned with what I have come to know as life that I just cannot take it anymore; when answers from out there no longer soothe me. Then I will turn within towards the faint voice that tries to speak to me every now and again.

Struggling through life uses up so much of my energy. It relentlessly tosses me around, fills me with concerns or self-doubt and keeps me entirely preoccupied. Often, I lose my hold, hit the ground hard and just do not want to be bothered with getting up anymore.

Life, I thought you were my friend. Maybe it's not about you at all. Perhaps, I am not being a friend to myself.

Maybe that is why I often feel lost, empty or frustrated. It isn't just me though. I often catch glimpses of a deep sorrow in the eyes of many other women as well. When will I find feelings of contentment and acceptance I so long to fill my belly with?

I sit self-entombed, grappling alone with stress, burdens and the crazy pursuit of material success and ambitions to be attained in a world I am not really happy in. I cannot seem to accept all this as complete reality. I sense somehow, that there is more. I just don't remember where to find it.

If I could just magically detach for a while, from all that keeps me chained, I could be free to journey up the mountain to where the wise woman sits wrapped in her ancient shroud of all knowingness that is timeless and constant.

I heard that her name is wisdom, Divine, feminine wisdom to be more exact. Rumors are murmured that she has become hidden, now unreachable, but many claim this to be an untruth. Some realize that she really resides within every woman whose incarnated soul resonates with her primordial femininity. They say she knows you, because she is you.

The Sacred Feminine at the core of my being, Her voice then must be my truth. The unheard part of me, the neglected part of me, the unclaimed part of me, the waiting part of me.

How is it that I forgot that within me lies her undiscovered world filled with my identity, filled with my beingness and my becoming? This world that wise woman beckons me to.

Yet, I keep turning away, avoiding this journey towards self-discovery. I simply do not remember how to go about it. I'm still not even sure if I am supposed to. Are there others I can ask? I also sense that if I turned towards her I would have to make some sort of commitment to her. I would want to, no I would yearn to, but who can I first speak to who has done the same?

I am continually drawn. This wise woman intrigues me, simply by her gentle, yet persistent tugging. She knows that which I need to know, and she is waiting for me to realize that what I am really looking for is me, all of me, my entire womanness.

So maybe, and I am only suggesting maybe, that in one of those moments of dark discontent I will choose to become a friend to myself by turning towards the voice of feminine awareness. I will cock my ear and try to catch her whisperings. One day...perhaps, if I am wise enough to make the time.

# 9

# The Third, Fourth and Fifth Dimensions

Due to the current dominance of separateness consciousness created by the lower ego, humankind has become fixated on the fleeting, physical outer life. Little attention is given to the infinite, abstract inner life of higher ego (higher mind) of the feminine principle. As a result, most humans have not yet evolved into the understanding of unified consciousness. It is way overdue. In our retarded evolution we do not comprehend the concept of working in **unison** to create positive change. But necessity is the mother of invention so we must become the change we wish to see around us and soon to halt the chaos and pain created by self-absorption and detachment.

If we look at the general public we see that the masses are not at this moment making great leaps and strides towards unity mindedness. Due to their deeply etched thought patterns they gravitate to such solutions as putting more locks on their doors in the face of growing violence to protect only themselves. They read about but do not adhere to Mother Earth's dilemma of pollution and toxic waste build-up. They don't give a hoot about the organic movement to halt the take-over of genetically modified foods or really sympathize with starving third world countries, the daily annihilation of various species in nature, nor the atrocities of wars fought in distant lands. This does not imply that they are not decent people. They have just not reached (by choice?) a higher level of thinking and acting that encompasses others. They live comfortably in their little box.

We are stuck in 3-D or third dimensional thinking, left-brain thinking, which is very physical world oriented. It is a headspace filled with the separateness ideals of "It's all about me, too bad about those others." You can see it in their actions or non-actions.

It is a disconnection from everyone and all that is, unless necessity or a heart tug initiates within them a moment of selflessness. People like this hold the entire race back from moving onto the fourth dimension.

The fourth dimension, associated with the Age of Aquarius, revolves around gaining greater intelligence through expanding our thinking in a different direction. It is about becoming more profound, less superficial. It is not about the current trend of mind racing anxiety resulting from useless information overload due to internet, twitter, facebook and so on. I am talking about a future that concentrates on development of the feminine or the right brain, which focuses on different types of intelligences we are barely using today. We find in the fourth dimension growing awareness, a deeper state of realization that we are all somehow interlocked and therefore what one says and does has an impact on all around us in the long run. It is the ripple effect revelation. Due to heightened insightfulness, thought and actions begin to be regulated by conscience. "Do unto others as you would expect them to do unto you," which by the way, is said to be the eleventh commandment. In esoteric writings it is stated that this is a level of consciousness that humanity should have already reached. It appears that we are lagging behind attaining this state of unity consciousness and as a result we are now on the edge of our own extinction. True women acknowledge and work comfortably with unity mindedness because it is ingrained in them.

Fifth dimension enlightenment of human beings is far in the future of humankind, except for a small percentage already there. For one thing, it is about our ability to recognize in our evolved state of unity consciousness, that there is our individual specialness as well. This is the soul uniqueness I keep speaking of. At this level of awareness we attain the honorable virtue selflessness. This level of awareness initiates a state of self-expansiveness whereby a person willingly enters selfless service as a humanitarian. In good conscience, they now use their special talents and abilities to primarily focus upon aiding people. Extending a hand as one's priority is the new tomorrow of fifth dimensional thinking. In order to become a Master one must first learn to humbly serve.

"What can I do to help make a positive contribution in the world?" one asks. Start simply by just taking the time to learn about the consequences of the small choices you make each day. Start caring and thinking about others. Again, it's a choice. This is definitely the first step towards attaining collective awareness and pushes us towards where we should all be at this time in humanity's progress.

Once people see that as individuals they do have a positive impact, they will be motivated to continue. Doing good and then feeling good afterwards is addictive because it leaves us with a sense of fulfillment. It is also contagious. Little steps away from selfness might in time lead to bigger steps. If not, just a lifetime of little steps goes a long way and eventually covers a lot of ground.

The reason I bring to your attention the three levels of consciousness is that it is an unavoidable part of the universal plan. We are all destined to continually heighten our vibrations toward higher consciousness while still remaining closely connected or rooted to the stable energies of Mother Earth. As I see it, most of us are doing neither at the moment. Since we are lagging behind in unity mindedness, retarding evolution by paralyzing ourselves in this state of selfness, the time has come for universal intelligence to step in and initiate movement for our own good, to loosen the grip of patriarchal thinking that keeps us static.

If this comes to pass, through universal force, many of us will perish. For catastrophes pushing us to realizations do not paint pretty outcomes. Remember, once again, the wisdom shared by the Mother Avatar I spoke of previously. She stated that at first the needed shift will be encouraged gently. If all of us whole-heartedly participate, it will be a relatively harmless unfolding into new consciousness. If we choose resistance, the push will become a force that will be dramatic to raise us to fourth dimensional thinking.

We are programmed in part as mammals and in part as divinely attuned souls. To move upward from animalistic tendencies into soulful consciousness is the answer to our survival. It is a natural pre-programmed progression. When a herd of animals have eaten all the shrubbery around them they move onward. It is their innate programming. We, on the other hand move upward, for within us is not just a need to survive but the need to evolve that pushes us along. To live comfortably in expanding populations we must raise ourselves up to fourth-dimensional thinking. To become respectful of the basic rights, needs and property of others will at least allow us to live more harmoniously amongst each other. Add to this respect for the Earth, and she will continue to sustain us so that we can thrive.

We live in a time when women's energy coming together will raise humankind to the next level of consciousness, the fourth dimension. It is not some feminist attitude that has concocted this theory in my head. I speak only as one spokesperson for the Goddess energy that is making Herself known in me. The imminent return to matriarchal ways is written in the stars.

However, there appears to be an underlying problem pertaining to our perception of time. We keep fooling ourselves into complacency by believing that we have ample time to dawdle. This is arrogance. Humanity is not indestructible. Vibrational tremors in the earth's aura, picked up by the sensitives to energy, indicate that a shift is well upon us. The message of peace woman Julie Morton Marr is timely. If you feel into it you will sense the urgency to make changes *now*.

In today's world we are caught up in the lower ego's need for self-gratification to the point of gluttony and unsettling insensitivity. We are far from the profoundness of the fourth dimension. Too bad, for this is why our troubles grow. At this moment most of us are at a complete loss as to even understanding the deeper meanings of the following three questions that define us from the inside out. Until we can grasp their meanings, we cannot possibly begin to answer these questions.

"What is my real worth if I lose my external identity and possessions?"

"What do I realize about myself that more fully defines me as special and gives me value as a unique soul?"

"What outpourings of positive contributions have I made, in selflessness, by extending myself to others or by making the world a better place to live in?"

When we can answer these questions in a way that gratifies the heart, then we will be well established in the fourth dimension and will possibly begin to have a foothold in the fifth. Until then, perhaps as a race that has fallen behind we should giddy-up a bit and become busier playing catch up.

# 10

## From Bud to Blossom

Ah woman! Such a splendid flower. Her warmth of heart makes her such a beautiful addition to humanity's garden. Everyone gravitates toward a person whose blossoming heart exudes love overflowing. This is real woman: soulful, deep, caring and nurturing.

I am blessed with wonderful women surrounding me of every age, in all shapes and sizes. When they are removed from life's burdensome responsibilities and left to breathe and relax into themselves, there is a radiance in their smiles that says "soul." Inner beauty is very attractive leaving everyone with a good, lasting impression. This beauty, so natural to woman, is often tarnished by the unworthiness she feels if she is not the sex symbol that a male directed society expects her to be.

From a very early age she is somehow expected to wear a frilly dress and ribbons in her hair to impress. In this way she is acceptable and praised. As if "isn't she a pretty little thing" is her defining feature, her aspiring destiny. Pre-programmed, she therefore spends her adolescence as well as her twenties, thirties, forties and even fifties fixated upon developing her exterior image.

Every woman in modernized societies works on being gorgeous rather than on being radiant from within. As she pre-occupies herself with her physical image, she neglects or plays down the importance of her true appeal, her resplendent heart. This is her real legacy to the world. She is not destined to be a sex symbol, rather a symbol of the heart. In a man's world she has been degraded to meet his needs. She is so much more than arm candy or body candy for that matter.

The majority of men (excluding those destined for prearranged marriages set up by their families) tend to choose women who turn heads. Few men seek women who are warm and loving as their first priority. So from the onset, confidence and self-esteem are crushed in women who are not born the bombshells of desire. There is a multi-billion dollar industry worldwide that lures us into the deception of needing to be good-looking, especially to the male. Hairstyling, false nails, pedicures, make-up, perfume, laser, waxing, Botox, skin tucks, liposuction, breast enhancement, surgical alterations, name brand fashion, high heels, dieting and million dollar smiles are all for the physical impression we hope to leave and be remembered by.

Yet, woman is not by nature shallow. Her deepness of spirit, her profound nature contradicts the manmade reality of superficiality she has conformed to as the propaganda of brainwashing continues. In a woman's world it would be entirely different. Yes, it is always nice to look good for it makes us feel good inside, but to feel good inside or good about ourselves should not depend upon how we look that day. We have bought into this absurdity of superficial appearances, especially in more affluent countries where what you have to show defines who you really are.

Recently, I attended a house party for the selling of wares where women, all friends of each other, were in their late forties. It struck me, as I listened, that seventy-five per cent of these women were working overtime to maintain their youthful appearance and beauty. The reason was because they were all just shy of age fifty which to them was horrifying. To stay looking good, at whatever cost, would be the deception that would fool the world and themselves that they were still "hot." Most had joined gyms with personal trainers. They were dyeing their graying hair. They were dressed to the nines with flawless make-up, false nails and spiked heels. All of them were frantically dieting. The most important question in their minds was "Do I still look youthful?"

Health is wealth and staying in shape is an energy boost and a boon to longevity; this however, was not the focus for Botox and facelifts dominated the conversation. Not one, not a one, wanted to accept let alone look their age. Youth and looks, the most important assets a woman could have, the only things worth relentlessly pursuing? I beg to differ. Aging is not an illness. Old people are not a disease of humanity.

Crossing the threshold of mid-life crisis into our fifties drives this home to the brainwashed, and not subtly I may add. Perhaps a woman's psychological crisis would not be so intense at this time in life, had we been taught early in the game that it is not what we look like but who we are on the inside that is of primary importance. If preening the inside would become the precedent, in this world of mislaid priorities, women would blossom earlier and longer. It is once again about balance, the personal balance of the whole self.

As universal laws would have it, our lessons must be learned. If not earlier in life, then definitely as we enter into the second half. Learn we must. Those of us who never get around to acknowledging our deeper womanness, our inner beauty and its gifts, age prematurely. The bud never fully opens and becomes the flower of our potential. We simply wither.

When youthfulness abandons us and sagging skin and age spots appear, we panic. We are forced then into an awareness that we should have reached earlier, had the wisdom from such places as elder women's circles been there to teach us.

The unchanging truth, generation after generation, is that woman's overall beauty resides in her heart. Living through your heart makes your eyes shine and the radiance of the aura you exude makes you timeless and ageless. Being truly woman is living through the joyful soul self as soulful woman should.

Every woman is a composite of love and wisdom (higher knowledge). As well, her soul possesses certain gifts and talents that enhance this. Upon this realization, she can bring forth into the world her specialness in a myriad of ways that fulfills her and exudes at the same time this timeless inner radiance I speak of. The true self is the ultimate beauty we are seeking. This ageless beauty comes from within, and that is where we have to go to find it.

Woman vibrationally is the higher representation of the Cosmic Feminine principle and is supposed to resonate overall beauty and wisdom. Her lower representation is child bearer and temptress to the male for procreation of the species. This is her animal, base nature. When the feminine energy incarnates into matter, she temporarily forgets her origins of higher self. She loses most of herself temporarily.

Eventually, unrest, inner conflict and identity issues plague her. This is the end result of her minimal knowledge of herself due to her lost identity, caused in part by the influence of men with their stereotypical perceptions of her. The pain of these constrictions eventually leads woman to profound questioning. Her innate programming will pull her back towards her deeper unconscious. Here, her true worth lays in waiting. For stroking the body might be where she begins her journey of identity but her destiny is to turn inward and return to stroking her soul.

It is therefore of importance, at some early point in woman's life, to make this realization before it is thrust upon her much later as she ages, unkindly. The shell we parade around in will weaken. It is fleeting. It is such a small part of our wholeness, yet in our forgetfulness, we know no other "me."

If we were all sightless, even partially blind, would it make any difference as to what we looked like apart from being clean? Visual perception belongs to the five external senses of the physical realm. The sixth sense of woman is an inner perception. We rarely use it, it is bypassed, yet it is of great importance.

I, for one, call upon my inner senses first to help me define and feel. I am either impressed, or not, by a person's energetic field. Their core, or inner vibrations, resonating outwards create this auric field that describes them to me. As a whole person, I try to connect on a whole level with others. From the initial, exterior connection I quickly move beyond that, inward. "Am I talking to an inflated ego or to humbleness, self-esteem or a person riddled with insecurity, inner strength or weakness of character, profoundness or superficiality?" Afterwards, I go even deeper and connect at the heart mind level. Is this person compassionate, kind, caring or am I looking at a closed heart that sends out a chill? The gift-wrap does not hide for long the real contents especially for a whole woman searching for a sense of completeness in another. For in the end, what leaves the greatest impression is not "having it all" but "having it all together."

As we become increasingly stuck on the physical and neglect other levels of our being, sex appeal, status and acquisition remain the scales we weigh people's worth upon. A wise woman once said to me, "The world is upside down. The ignorant rule while those with great wisdom, in their humbleness, obey." I call it the absurdity of chaos.

The whole woman can break apart this cycle of utter nonsense, for she has an inner sense that comes from highest values, in her deepest place of knowing. Again, she just has to remember it. When arrived at the uninhibited state of her completeness she will no longer be brainwashed by half-truths or false perceptions. It is then that she will be able to fulfill her destiny by raising her energy up and emanating the powers associated with her inner, radiant beauty. Now that is what really makes heads turn!

# 11

# On Being Naturally Woman

A rose, by any other name, is still a rose. The color red, be it crimson, scarlet or cherry remains red, and a woman, encouraging or denying her feminine power still remains programmed as fully woman.

Everything has unalterable core properties that define it. In cosmic creation, a specific energetic vibration is the blueprint that precedes its physical manifestation. It can be likened to specific codes found in D.N.A. A rose, therefore, cannot over time on its own transform into a daisy nor can a woman deny her real self and attempt to become manlike in her characteristics. Perhaps she will succeed temporarily, but at some point by tampering with her core vibrations, she will fall victim to inner conflict, malaise or illness.

In today's world, especially in the gladiators' arena known as business, women are attempting to mutate, actually disconnecting from their femininity. They are developing male-like behaviorisms as they compete in the work place. Sadly, they bring that "new me" home with them. There is no question that adapting is a valuable tool of survival. But this is hardly the case here, for women who morph into manlike behavior are not preserving their species; rather, they are further de-womanizing half of humanity.

Having been around long enough to now gracefully admit that I am a crone (which simply means wise woman with plenty of life knowledge) I have observed that a large number of females, especially between the ages of 20 and 45, are in identity crisis. Often forced to enter areas in the work force, which can be competitive and aggressive, they develop male characteristics to hold onto their jobs. The stress and demands in this arena only accelerates male behaviorism in them. Over time, these women become more insensitive, arrogant, impatient, inflexible, aggressive and hardened. I wonder if they even realize what is happening to them? Others are trying consciously to become equal in man's world by acting like men, which simply makes them neither a man nor a woman.

In a man's world, especially in that of the workplace, women adapt or go against their natural, programmed tendencies. In North America droves of women have abandoned the home, leaving empty shells that once exuded their vibrant presence.

In the spirit of modernization, or let's be frank, capitalism, women have lost vital aspects of themselves for the natural environment of woman remains the home front, especially once there are children, and the outside work jungle is the natural habitat of the male. Let me explain the facts before the working woman reading this slams this book shut and calls me archaic. Since the beginning it has been man, due to his physical core properties as *hunter and provider* who has left the home daily to battle the elements in order to bring home the bacon. Woman as *nurturer and caregiver*, her core properties, has comfortably stoked the home fires while doing the other million things that provide for a healthy home environment. This created a nice balance that provided for all the family's physical and nurturing needs as a self-sustained unit.

Today, the business world is the modern jungle that man is left to venture out into daily in order to provide for his family. It has been created for him and by him so that he can continue to demonstrate those primal needs as hunter and provider. Take this away from him and he withers. Just look at all the unemployed men in the United States as a result of the current economic crisis. During interviews for a television documentary, all confessed to feeling totally emasculated because they prove their manhood primarily through their job positions and their ability to provide for and therefore protect their loved ones. Like it or not, the work world is an extension of male core properties just like the home is the extension of the woman's. The exception might be when a woman starts up a small business that is specific to her creative energies. This entity called the business is much less competitive and stressful in nature for it is, in its uniqueness, created by the woman's extension of herself, and attracts to her, her clientele. Call it a personalized, creative extension of herself that generates income.

Beware, however, that if this business that starts out as a personal expression of self grows too big or becomes franchised, a highly competitive energy replaces that which originally was its attractive drawing card; its specialness is lost. Its uniqueness, its personality, is altered from the woman's way into the man's way of doing business.

Perhaps for the sake of preserving the "woman energy" in her business, the motto "small is best" should be seriously considered. Bigness in business goes hand in hand with the male perspective of doing things. The innate need of males is to be the dominant conqueror, with the most assets or territory to give them a sense of power and control. This feeds the businessman's driving force, or lower ego, that thrives on acquisition and status.

So business competes and corporations grow as an extension of the male's needs and will naturally eliminate the threat of competition with aggression and indifference. Takeovers and buying the other business out feeds his conqueror nature. For women to survive in man created atmospheres such as these, which are fiercely competitive, they automatically must become manlike or they will be eliminated. In the man's world, "survival of the fittest" or "dog eat dog" mottos are the prime directives, especially in larger companies as they protect their territory. This attitude of self over others is spilling into everyday life, it is no longer exclusive to the work place and women working under these influences adapt, or morph, to hold onto their positions. In today's world, this state of being keeps being augmented by the drive of consumerism frenzy; hook the consumer at any cost to your conscience.

Perhaps, to preserve and augment their feminine core properties, women should seriously give thought to magnifying their innate characteristics by pursuing careers that enhance who they are and leave the business jungle to the male. The list of prestigious jobs suited for woman is extensive, not at all limited, and these are not fiercely competitive or male like, going against her natural character as non-aggressive. Some of my suggestions include: careers in the healing arts, health professionals, nutritionists, environmental workers, workshop facilitators, artisans, school teachers and principals, caregivers, herbalists, chefs, caterers, gardeners, events planner, designers, interior decorators, florists, horticulturists, organic farmers, creative artists, authors, editors, beauty professionals, nannies, psychologists, spiritual psychotherapists, counselors, etc. These are but a few professions which would enhance the core attributes of true woman, not compromise it.

Why not begin now to embrace our collective womanness and live according to its energy? It would be easier for females to be just naturally themselves. To keep adapting to what a male run society wants us to be is simply unnatural. Unnatural is uncomfortable and stressful. Isn't it just easier to be that which was universally programmed into us? Or do we go against common sense and continue to conform to accommodate man's reality, or half of whole reality being forced upon us.

For some reason, woman's ways and woman's wisdom from our elder crones have stopped being passed down, especially to post World War Two women. This lack of information has left a void in women's identity and they are now incomplete and weakened by it. Instead, they spend all their time preening the physical self or they fill that void of incompleteness with full time jobs to give them financial worth and purpose. Working is not in itself the problem. It is, however, a poor substitute for self-identification. It is causing mutating in many women as they become more manlike or weaker versions of the Feminine Principle.

To support this, I will share one story of a woman and her personal mid-life crisis. Since the age of thirty-five, this woman has been a prominent bank manager in a very male influenced business, which focuses entirely on the acquisition of money. There is nothing at all in this profession that promotes one's feminine energy. Yet, her job has become her sole identity. She mutated, even as a mother, for her children – an extension of herself – were raised by a nanny. Now at age fifty-four, somehow she has become totally miserable. All she yearns to do, from that deeper place within, is to quit her job and return to the home and live her life differently.

Her inner programming is trying to re-direct her, trying to rebalance her. The need to become yourself, at any cost, is what mid-life crisis is all about. It is about completing the journey of self-discovery.

Whether this woman can liberate herself from her current identity associated with high salary and status is left to be seen. This is the type of struggle that each of us face under different circumstances when the yearning starts pulling us in the right direction. If this woman does not return to her authentic self and live the rest of her life expressing her true womanness in a multitude of ways, including finding a job that expresses the true self, then her unnatural state of being will bring on psychological and physical deterioration or gradual self-destruction. Unhappiness, due to a sense of unfulfillment or loss of self, has a tendency to do that.

Modernized woman is letting go of her deeper identity, and in so doing, she has removed herself from her most important role in society, that of being the very heart of it. Is she really any longer the devoted heartbeat of her family, her home and her community? Sometimes, some are, but that is just not good enough. Why? Simply because the backlash is that society, ironically, is fast becoming heartless!

A woman's way is really an influential heavy hand in the affairs of home, family and community. Her role and her presence are of paramount importance in keeping these three crucial areas that create bonding in society from dissolving.

Where I live, we pride ourselves in the North American way, which is that of individualism. In its exaggeration it has become isolation from others due to separateness consciousness. As a result, our society has become fragmented. We suffer, often unknowingly, from feelings of aloneness as we mourn an inner lose, that feeling of connectedness that humans thrive on.

Before the age of Industrialization, which has become the age of Capitalism, women stayed at home. They were the backbone of their communities, present, involved and interconnected one home to the next, giving meaning to the word COMMUNITY as communal. Now since the homes are vacant, so are the neighborhood streets, like ghost towns.

Long ago, Thomas Jefferson voiced the following warning "DO NOT industrialize." He feared that family solidarity would be severely compromised and that the face of society's structure would become fragmented. How prophetic!

In a local newspaper, a mayor of an upper middle class-to affluent neighborhood in Quebec spoke out about mounting vandalism and theft in his municipality. I quote from this paper:

The problem is in the way our society has shifted and become re-structured. Both parents are now working and their children and teenagers are left to wander the streets and create trouble. As they are let out of schools between 2:30 and 3:00 p.m. they are left unsupervised and are often not accountable for their whereabouts from that time until 6:00 p.m. when parents come home.

Finally, it is being pointed out blatantly that absentee, therefore, delinquent parenting is a large part of delinquent behavior in their children. This is fast becoming a societal issue everywhere as we neglect our primary jobs as caretakers in pursuit of jobs that create affluence.

Woman, taking her position as the heartbeat of family, home and community, is simply honoring her core nature. What we have forgotten is that this is her primary position in society at least when she is in the period of raising children and it is certainly a position to be very proud of!

I applaud Thomas Jefferson's insightfulness and I mourn the misplaced or lost woman of modern times.

Creativity, nurturing and leading with the heart are parts of female core properties, just as protector, aggressor and leading with the lower ego mind are core properties of the male's makeup. Each has its purpose and territory. No amount of external modernization can alter these inner workings, for we will always be pulled back to our true selves eventually.

Now, during the cosmic resurgence of the feminine principle, women, more than ever before, must faithfully encourage their identities by becoming aware of the Cosmic Mother's blueprint. The power of the woman's way, her natural tendencies, cannot be subdued, denied or avoided. Empty homes, dissolving families and loss of community inter-activeness are part of the sufferings of modernized societies that have become too yang.

Many women, but not enough, still remain true to their natures. Many more are starting to realize the need to return to it. Keep an eye out as more and more women break away from the unnatural order created by patriarchal dominance. Women will move forward only by moving back to their primordial roots.

At this point I remind you that going back to ancient ways of established truths does not imply being house bound, or once again being tied to a stove with apron strings while holding tightly onto a scrubbing board. We all do move forward with the times. Progress is the antidote for stagnation. However, we must remember to take these established truths with us, so as to keep laying the same solid foundations to build ourselves upon. Woman should never be without her full identity and deeper purpose, whatever she chooses to become.

A multi-dimensional woman is, in essence, a multi-task woman, without the stress. For in her completeness she owns and directs her power and her life with a comfortable sense of certainty. A woman who knows who she really is makes choices that resonate with her, not against her. "Just be comfortably you" is a great beginning towards unraveling the mysteries of the real self that will allow you to live all aspects of your life in this fashion.

A woman's personal and professional life should always be an expression of her womanly strengths, as well as her individual skills and talents. Her life should exude her own nurturing energy in the home and outside of it and should never be put on a back burner or suppressed due to her wrong lifestyle choices. There is absolutely no reason why a woman's touch cannot enhance work places that can only profit from her deep-rooted sense of self. Rather than accommodate she should find work where her womanness can freely flow. I say this because, bear in mind, there are certain jobs ill-suited for a woman, just as there are certain occupations ill-suited for man's energy.

There is no need to elaborate upon what these are for either side, for as the reader studies charts A and B, these blueprints will serve as guidelines to help figure out what each polarity is more naturally suited for. Nothing is gained by forcing one's foot into a shoe that will never really be comfortable. Why would we even want to?

Remembering the egg and the sperm story, we realize that within every human are traits of both energies waiting to develop fully as we evolve. At this time in our history, the male properties are more dormant in the female and the feminine principle is more dormant in the male. Females are thus meant to fully represent the feminine consciousness and men the male cosmic consciousness. Until woman truly gets reacquainted with her feminine principle and expresses her identity she remains lost woman and full expression of the Feminine Divine is stunted. It is true that there are men and women who have mastered the use of right- and left-brain intelligence and appear to be more androgynous in thinking, attitudes and actions. For the most part this future type of human is still relatively rare in humanity.

Once women again know who they are on a collective level, accept it and become it, they will realize that their worth is not based upon money, status, profession or prettiness. The thumbprint they will then strive to leave behind will be the vibrations of their *heartprint*.

# 12

# The Sisterhoods and Women's Circles

From women's primitive tribal gatherings, rites of passage ceremonies, Goddess and nature rituals to more current quilting and sewing circles, ladies' Sunday teas or girls' night out, there is an underlying theme.

Since the earliest of times, women have had a need to come together in groups to bond and support one another. It might appear to be just a girls' thing, but only on the surface. The focal point is their innate need for interconnectedness through the traditions of the sisterhood; a place and opportunity to communicate feelings, share that which needs sharing and embrace femaleness. It goes much deeper than merely socializing now and again.

As modern woman suffers from lost woman's syndrome, one of her personal casualties is that she is out of touch with her core need to unite with other females on this deep level. This disconnection from self and her comrades leaves her alone to struggle endlessly through major passages of her life that sculpt her womanness.

The current aerobic class, group jog or workplace is not conducive to this bonding experience. Women now escape to sport clubs which are competitive, workshops which are random, yoga classes which are solitary experiences; and let's not forget the mall which simply fills an otherwise empty day.

Women are beginning to buckle from the lack of reinforcement which comes from the alliance of sisterhoods and women's circles, so they reach for tranquillizers, sleeping pills and grapple with anxiety disorders, stress, addictions, depression and over and underweight conditions. They cope, suffer in silence, or lean upon therapists. Eventually, they fall victim to such women ailments as burnout, nervous breakdown, severe mood swings, chronic fatigue syndrome and fibromyalgia, or settle into an ongoing state of helplessness. As they lose sight of the self and each other, this weakens them both individually and collectively.

The support systems found in sisterhoods or women's circles of the past replenished hope and energy, offered direction around life's looming obstacles and provided a haven of acceptance where one could laugh and let go, learn and be nurtured. These groups reminded us that we do not stand alone for we share similar experiences. My mother once put it nicely when she said, "Although the wallpaper in our kitchens is different, the life experiences are the same." There appears to be comfort in knowing that we suffer and rejoice collectively while treading on similar paths clinging onto one another.

Obscure hamlets, villages and even towns are fast disappearing as large cities encroach upon them; with it leaves the sense of cohesiveness found within them and the towns' women that organized celebrations or rites of passage ceremonies as part of fellowship. It appears that a sense of togetherness encouraged people to interact and support each other on a more regular basis. Women remained involved and worked their magic. In their communities they took charge of such things as teaching, celebrations, social get-togethers and people's personal needs. They also kept a sharp eye on their neighbors, busy-bodies at times, but concerned citizens as well.

Today, the family and extended family are all that remain of groups that continue these traditions amongst themselves. In family, we still find a common bond and in it we find women at different levels of development such as grandmothers, mothers, aunts, older sisters, teenagers and finally young children. Those who are the eldest need to remember to come together periodically to perform rites of passage for their younger loved ones. Yet, even in families, I am noticing that initiations and support groups are falling by the wayside, even in this last stronghold of supposed togetherness.

One reason might be that these ancient ways of women have stopped being handed down. For another, families are spread apart. Women are often left struggling to raise their children alone due to distancing. With this, and the forgotten ways of ancient bonding, even family clans are not as tight as they once were.

For woman the need to bond is due to a soul urge that reminds her to maintain interconnectedness as a spiritual being who is, for a time, taking part in the human experience. Even if we do not like to socialize with people, which is just an extension of our outer personalities, the core urge remains.

In families it is predominantly the woman that is the social director. She does the calling and catching up, the inviting, the festive family gatherings and the remembering of everyone's birthday. She co-ordinates get-togethers with friends, spouse's friends and her young children's friends. As well, she hob-knobs with her surrounding neighbors.

Men, on the other hand, just seem to stand back while their female partners do what is natural for them. Generally men only extend themselves minimally in other people's lives. They lack interconnecting skills, being of a detached nature more so as they age, to the extent of sometimes being not only indifferent but becoming reclusive as well.

Even though women still tend to be more social or involved with others, the deeper soul to soul bonding in groups is not only not flourishing; it is on life support! This soul urge that reminds us to connect to the Cosmic Feminine and other females is being ignored. Perhaps it is simply because we have forgotten how to because the trend is disappearing. This coming together preserves the Great Mother's identity within us by allowing it to be re-born through us each time we create a women's circle.

Young girls, as early as primary school and until their late twenties, especially in today's age tend to move in small groups. They learn about life, each other and themselves from these clusters or cliques by intimately sharing each other's experiences. They are often inseparable due to this innate need. This loyalty to the group allows for individual growth and awareness through the collective experience. Common joys and shared dilemmas unite on a soul level that bonds them for life.

My own adolescent memories were stored on the dusty shelves of my mind until I observed my nineteen-year-old daughter's patterns of behavior. Through her, I am reminded as to how I used to act at her age. She, as well as her female friends, still honor naturally the lost art of the sisterhood. For as of yet, their lives remain uncluttered with the "have to" responsibilities of a demanding lifestyle that eventually re-programs us into an unnatural way of living in a man's world.

It is only as we move well into adulthood that we become totally absorbed in physical responsibilities and become torn away from time spent nurturing relationships with kindred spirits. Eventually, this neglect brings on the ills associated with separateness. Sadly, we are kept so busy developing the external image of keeping up with the Joneses that we are fully hypno-tized by capitalism. In less ambitious times, which were also less transient times, there was more opportunity to remain linked and blend with other females.

Today, as always, women lose at least half of their me-time due to spousal and family responsibilities. They also still work inside as well as now outside of the home. Time is more limited. Add to this, that in a transient society it is common to move away from our roots of origin or relocate to the other side of the sprawling metropolis we were raised in. In either scenario one loses touch with those who, in our developing years of youth, helped shape our budding identity. Our deeper needs, in part the recollection of our identities, have been waylaid by our frenzied, weary, overwrought adult lives. Who has time left to be a part of a sisterhood?

It is easy to see how and why the crumbling of women's circles happened for females that got caught up in a man's way of living. Modernization has created an epidemic of stressed out, isolated women on the run. It is not necessarily due to overload. Women have always worked from dawn to dusk in their homes or in the fields, while tending to families. Our days, since the beginning, have been consumed by chores and responsibilities. Even today, though our time is not devoured by mending clothes and then manually scrubbing them, our time is now taken up in the workplace. Since nothing has changed, why are we more stressed?

Partly, it may be due to the accelerated pace of insane work lifestyles that leave us often with a sense of inner frustration. It is also due to the lack of an intact support system that would somehow help life remain more sane and manageable.

Perhaps if we reinstated the women's groups that sustain sisterhoods, at least part of the problem of stressed out, disjointed women could be solved and we could wean ourselves off all the pills that keep us from falling apart. Again, I am not talking here about having two or three friends to unload on.

For readers between the ages of thirty to late forties, these sororities I suggest might not appeal to you, for you don't sense a need for them. This is because, at this young stage of your lives you are in a state of busyness, emitting a false sense of completeness. Your busyness suppresses that inner need you do not have time to acknowledge. But to ignore or more tragically let go of the thread that binds all women together sets us up for personal distress in our futures once we are not so crazy-busy.

For overall health is emotional, mental, spiritual and physical well-being all rolled into one. Things of inner substance invisible to the eye such as contentment, joyousness, positiveness and feelings of self-worth feed health. To this we can add minimal stress, true friendships, a sense of security through belonging and ongoing enthusiasm for life. Let us not forget the need for group hugs that warm more thoroughly than any cup of hot cocoa.

Women's circles created through friendship, family ties or just randomness provide us with these intangibles that have infinite worth, yet no monetary value. Of course, they are not the only place where we can acquire that which is vital to our beingness but it is one more place where it should be readily available. For women, more so than men, are drawn to seeking deeper meaning to the shallowness of life through bonding.

Alliances of women initially lead to comradery then onwards to lasting friendships. Tried and true bonds offer a variety of delightful desserts. Women, it seems, can quite easily connect deeply on a soul level once trust has been established. With it comes the perks of sisterhoods that accentuate life.

In our hardships, which are so much a part of everyday living, we struggle today as lone warriors fighting what appears to be endless battles. It is we against the world. Would it not be easier if we could find solace in the comfort of others and somehow work together through an intimate circle of warmth and kindness?

As well, it would aid us to find hope and encouragement through fellowship when needed, by those who actually care and understand because they too are women. Finally, also to be able to have a sanctuary of non-judgment where one can belly laugh or cry whole-heartedly leaving us feeling once again good about life or ourselves. This is some of the magical medicine found in women's groups.

The second half of life, which can last fifteen to forty-five years, arrives sooner than we expect. Before we know it we are in peri-menopause, a time when everything shifts not only physically but in our psyches, in our energy levels and, as a result, in our lifestyles and attitudes as well.

We begin to grow discontent and weary with what was and

still is our life. We have outgrown it. As our abstract and physical molecules are being re-arranged by an unseen hand, we no longer want to be involved simply with the "same old, same old." We yearn for outer change to complement the changes taking place within us, even if we are unsure as to what that will be. While our bodies are rapidly altering, a new cycle of becoming is also being born as we enter our fullness of maturity.

Understandably, we often feel lost during this transformation and have no one or nothing to hang on to for a sense of solidness; the solution appears to be anti-depressants. Entering the second half of our lives is a radical shift. It is similar to when we went from childhood into adolescence, except in a different way. One is about finding individualized identity, the other is about attaining maturity through completeness. We return to where we left off, taking the bud of individualized identity and encouraging it to become fully mature. It is, therefore, just as important as it was in adolescence to have that supporting group in which to share our experiences of transition.

Having the insight to keep our women connections intact is as important as instinctively having taken care of our physical health in preparation for the benefits later on in life. Most of us do neither, for we live in the moment. Psychological well-being is as important as physical well-being, especially when adjusting to major life transitions. It makes the process more fluid and fills us with positive anticipation to minimize our struggles.

Older women caught up in these changes often find that the only connections they maintain with other women are with one or two friends or a sister. Though these life-long connections are invaluable, this is not the sisterhood I speak of for it is incomplete. At some point during life passage transitions we find ourselves coping with profound feelings of disconnection or aloneness that one or two friends cannot soothe.

The true you is partly the collective you that once realized removes all exterior boundaries and leaves women unified in a deeply identical, cosmic sense. This needs to be developed. If nowhere else, this is available in sisterhoods of groups of women. These circles must again widen and the rituals of bonding be revived for woman's overall wellness. It is about her healing, stability, empowerment and joyfulness of being.

Looking at these circles in yet another way, sororities creating alliance are also one approach towards alleviating the mistreatment and contempt towards women that is still obvious today, and incomprehensible. This is not just the reality of the uneducated in distant lands, it is the behavior of the ignorant and can be happening in your neighbor's home.

The root of the word *ignorance* is to ignore and can mean different things. It can imply unlearned, unaware, unconscious or misinformed. It can also mean choosing voluntarily to not acknowledge for self-serving purposes, or it can be resistance to truth due to fear of outside consequences. These forms of ignorance, by choice or by circumstance, create the rampant mistreatment of women. In fact, it is endemic in societies where men wield control because they have been taught that they are superior. This type of patriarchal thinking is not only found in third world, undeveloped countries.

Newspapers in every part of the world are filled with stories of the despicable behavior of men who stalk, assault, intimidate and murder their wives and random women. While this type of behavior is against the law in more advanced societies such as in North America, these laws do not seem to deter men who refuse to develop equality consciousness and are comfortable with femicide.

Many countries still keep their women ignorant. For example, in that ignorance often rooted in fear, there are still inhumane rituals performed on young women readying themselves for marriage, all for the self-centered demands of domineering male cultures. This is especially the case in parts of Africa. The rites women are forced to perform on other women are done through submission. They are controlled, trapped and kept uneducated.

Recently, a poll about women was conducted by the Thomson Reuters Foundation. This foundation registered in the U.S. and the United Kingdom in 1982 offers legal and humanitarian news and information worldwide. The polls theme was how well protected the rights of women were as egalitarian to men. Nineteen countries with strong economies were targeted. Canada rated number one, Germany was second, the United Kingdom was third, fourth and fifth were Australia and France. The lowest at number nineteen was India, eighteen was Saudi Arabia and Indonesia, South Africa and Mexico were rated as seventeen, sixteen and fifteen.

The top three were high in safeguarding women and their rights to education, health care, work, property ownership, political participation and protection against violence and slavery. Any country from number four downwards was qualified as doing rather poorly and numbers fifteen to nineteen had abysmal disrespect for equality towards the female, viewing them as unworthy creatures. While a few of the countries mentioned had a charter of rights that included women, it is obvious that many had no such regulations due to imbedded, archaic religious and cultural beliefs. As a result, thousands of women die annually due to brutality in these countries, which are conveniently dismissed as tragic accidents to cover up the unacceptable truth.

In time, women such as these will need our help to set them free. Women living in first world civilizations are still fighting their own smaller battles. But since we are, for the most part, more liberated we can add our voices to those of other stifled women and together become deafeningly loud. We need to proclaim in unison (such as through women's groups) our resentment to the abuse of women in any culture.

Before that can happen woman needs to reclaim herself collectively. Having more freedoms and opportunity, women living in Western democratic countries can rise to the occasion as spiritual warriors for those who cannot. They can begin the process by connecting once again in groups to each other to solidify power. This cannot help but lead to a force of greater female consciousness as growing sisterhoods link into the cosmic feminine principle. Women owe it to their diminishing true identities and to each other to pull together and rescue one another.

Women's circles are a great beginning point to encourage inner growth through self-awareness. They allow us a place to take pride in our womanhood. Furthermore, it is also a place to explore the ancient ways of women that reveal her greater purpose in the scheme of things. Soul to soul, heart to heart, hand to hand, she must now connect. For by reaching outwards she is also reaching inwards.

The North American trend of separateness and self-centeredness has led to a chronic overall state of detachment.

As long as there are women there will always be the ways of the woman, some of which are the age-old ceremonies found in the sisterhoods. If they become dormant through neglect, or if the wisdom they impart has been stifled by societies intent on weakening the feminine, in time they will always resurrect. For while on the outside we are subject to patriarchal interpretations to life we will be led back as often as necessary to the timeless truths of cosmic order through balance.

The energies of duality, yin and yang, are continuously active in the ongoing creation of cosmic evolution. If we look back upon our own history we see periodic surges of the feminine force creating balance. One such period was the previously mentioned Paleolithic era of old Europe. Another was the time in early Egypt when priestesses were revered for their higher knowledge or wisdom. While the feminine consciousness appears to sleep and then fully awakens at different times, it is simply in keeping with the cosmic plan of progression.

One way of re-awakening the Cosmic Mother is by re-initi-ating women's groups and together seeking out ancient teachings that are always readily available to those in search. By networking with other groups intent on doing the same, an abundance of information can be exchanged. Available are also a surge of current writings by women in the know who have modernized ancient texts by inserting modern psychological and psychotherapeutic perspectives, and their intuitive knowledge. Books, CDs and workshops now abound in preparation for a great shift to female consciousness already under way.

Women's groups can focus on any aspect that is naturally an extension of who they are. They can explore holistic health techniques, organic gardening, wholesome food preparation, environmental concerns, mothering, soul work, community projects, creative expression and other options that promote and augment their diversity.

There are also groups to be formed for the sole purpose of participating in rites and celebrations. These rituals honor life, nature, self, others and the universe. There are also many books written on the how-to's of recreating these ancient celebrations.

At first glance these ceremonies may appear outdated to today's 21st-century woman, but upon closer investigation they reveal profound messages and insights that even today are invaluable. The rites themselves can be modernized while still retaining their core purpose. For example, the celebration of the four seasons can be performed in any manner that follows basic guidelines. However we choose to do it, even with a modern twist, will leave us with a genuine connection to Mother Earth.

In any procedure, we must not lose sight of the message. With the four season celebrations, these cycles mimic the recurring four seasons in our own lives. Through these rituals we come to acknowledge and work with the season we are personally experiencing at the time.

The spring cycle refers to a time, once again, for new beginnings, new decisions and new direction. It is about a commitment to a change that will enhance our lives because we choose to create this change. Summer is the uplifting period when we start to see the fruits of our labour actualized as the new direction we took with our lives starts to manifest. Autumn is the harvest of rewards, the gifts of steadfast perseverance; it is about arriving. Lastly, winter is the welcome reprieve after the harvest we created has been reaped. The pendulum swings from full activity into dormancy, or inactivity for the sake of rest and reflection on future projects. Then, once again, when we are rejuvenated and the next project is in place, we bring on spring once more. Age has no bearing on the seasons we create perpetually in our lives.

Each cycle or each season can last for months or drag out for years, depending on our commitment to make it a reality or our resistant willfulness that resists change. Specific rites associated with the four seasons reinforce the need for these cycles to continue uninhibited in our lives.

Another rite, the moon ceremonies, helps us understand our emotional natures. The moon resonates with the Divine Feminine or yin associated with emotionality and spirituality as base components. The sun resonates with yang.

The lunar cycle ebbs and fills, culminating in the full moon, influencing women's emotions in the process. Rare men who have developed their emotional natures are also subject to the moon's magnetic pull. Luna is associated with woman's ability to feel deeply and respond with sensitivity.

During the phases of the black moon and the full moon, negative emotions peak. They are unrealized or untamed feelings due to unresolved issues and personal conflict. Hence it is laughable, in its accuracy, for men or your teenagers to dub you during this trying time as a "raving luna-tic!" For it appears we have temporarily lost our minds to our emotions. We have. During the dark nights of a woman's emotional cycle, negative feelings arise in the forms of fearfulness or insecurity, moodiness or irritability, anger or rage, sorrow or depression and anxiety or self-doubt.

Participating collectively in lunar rites of passage during these phases brings awareness that all this is normal to a degree and that all females are under the same influence at exactly the same time.

Luna is actually our aid for in order to work towards our own inner harmony we are being forced to meet our dark side over and over again. Lunar cycles allow us opportunity to examine our *whole* selves by really looking at our other side, the one we are often ashamed to acknowledge. This shadow side is alive, very much a part of us and deserves to be recognized, for it is a composite of our own limitations and weaknesses. To meet them is to know them. To know them is to challenge them. To challenge them is to dissolve these limitations one by one.

Partaking in rituals such as these reminds us over and over again to face our dilemmas and move through them.

Essentially, female or male peer groups in teen-hood, help the adolescent make a smoother transition from dependent child into self-assured adult. Well organized youth groups or social circles encourage the developing young adult to gradually step away from the guardian parent and learn to comfortably make decisions on their own, not through harsh rebellion. It is for this reason that peers become so much more important to teens at this time than loving parents. Simply put, it is a natural part of growing up and independence.

Once into adulthood, young moms in groups can learn the art of mothering without having to rely solely on remembering the ways of their own mothers. In circles, information and encouragement are exchanged. Also, they learn about community resources that can aid mother and child.

Older women find comfort in sharing experiences of menopause, empty nests and fading youth with a group that is in the same place as they are. Finally, senior females need to come together in friendship circles to share reflections on life, good conversation and group activities.

At any age, there are groups to be formed to pursue common interests, or for light-hearted fun There is also the possibility of circles forming to practice ancient rituals and investigate deeper wisdoms that explain the feminine principle.

Finally, there are the basic celebrations of life, the coming together to honor traditions or special occasions. Some women's groups exist only for this important purpose and are the catalysts that bring families or community together on a regular basis.

If these varying types of circles once again flourish, these sisterhoods will become like extended family, a safe haven of acceptance where one is welcome as a part of the whole. It can be likened to the warm embrace of your mother, except that it is tenfold, for it is the embrace of many women. There is no greater feeling than this.

What we wholeheartedly put into our group determines what it will give us back and what it becomes. Each group's focus is as unique as its participants. In its diversity it should retain one collective property; personalities aside, *it needs to be a nurturing, accepting space.* Keeping that unifying thought in mind, we can all benefit immensely from the whole experience.

# 13

## The Climb Through Womanhood

What is a plateau? What is a threshold in life unfolding?

Each major plateau is a life passage in a human being's journey towards self-actualization. In womanhood, the four basic ones are: the adolescent stage, followed by the period when woman chooses a mate, then there is motherhood, and lastly crone-hood. As we pass through each we learn more about who we really are and, in the end, upon the depth of those realizations we develop a higher level of maturation physically, mentally, emotionally and spiritually.

The intent of life's journey is to really get to know oneself and in that knowledge to become the best we possibly can be, living true to ourselves and helping others through the spirit of unity. Each life passage is developing us individually, while strengthening the collective self.

By trudging the outward journey through one life experience after the other and coupling that with the inward journey of inner reflection, we travel a tricky dual path. This has to be because we are dual in nature, being Divine spirit inhabiting a physical body. In a long life we are rewarded with invaluable life knowledge and street smarts to glean from. By pursuing our inner journey we are rewarded with soul or higher wisdom. We also are given insights about the collective self. The more we learn, the more tools we gain to master each passage in life with its challenges to promote growth.

The plateaus I mention in the following section are intended not only to build the human side of us but to ensure development of the soul self and the collective self as well.

A threshold is likened to the final stepping-stones that move us up from the previous plateau to the next one. Each step on the threshold is designed to prepare and equip us with what is needed to tackle the challenges of the awaiting plateau. It is the generations that go before us that must build these steps for the newcomers and then help them up onto each one.

As young children, we focus on everything except our sexuality. Until the ages of six or seven, we perform as androgynous beings, reminded once in a while to be either "a good little girl" or "a good little boy." Generally, we are reminded as to what sex we are for we are encouraged to play with either girl or boy toys. We automatically mimic Mom if we are female and Dad if we are male, as our role models of womanhood or manhood, respectively. However, most of our young life is absorbed in just playing. If there are no girls around, we play, without inhibition or distinction with boys and vice-versa.

When does this defining moment arrive, when girls really start paying attention to their sexuality? One can comfortably say it begins around age eleven, in grades five or six, when the body is entering puberty. Even before the actual hormonal, physical changes are obvious, there develops an awareness; with it, we start to have feelings and attractions for the opposite sex.

Silly little crushes, first loves, innocent flirtations, giggling in the corner as to who likes who, and a new sensation of awkwardness when talking to boys, are all indications that a shift out of childhood is occurring. These stirrings are the beginnings of the wonderful journey through womanhood.

# 14

# The Climb: Threshold One

There are four major plateaus in womanhood which I will elaborate on in this section. While every woman searching for her completeness travels the same journey, she does so on different paths. She stops, however, on the same embankments as her travelling sisters. These important thresholds we pause upon give us opportunity to bond with other women for a while before we all move separately, yet collectively, onward. We can be certain that at every stage of our maturing we will encounter many women in exactly the same circumstances if we look about and reach out.

Although there is comfort in company as we anticipate together the next major plateau, there is little information to prepare us, for our peers in waiting are also unlearned due to lack of experience. We only know about where we have come from, not about where we are yet to go.

Then, who provides the map, so to speak? Who explains the way? Perhaps we can ask an older woman for insights. One older woman's shared experiences is simply one viewpoint. This is why I encourage the revival of women's groups. If those who travelled along the way previously would continue, in tradition, to come together to help younger women, transitions onto each plateau would probably be smoother. It would be a relief to know that emotional re-assurance is always available as we transit from one plateau to another.

The first plateau is teen-hood, its threshold is the onset of puberty. At least physically, "I am woman" defines teen years for the female, as nature sculpts her body into that identity. In time as you add the complementary clothes, hairstyles and accessories, you begin to accept the first level of adulthood.

My own experiences, as well as those of my female peers, during this phase were not remembered as a passage supported by ceremony, warmth and welcome or lengthy instruction. Rather we huddled together, exchanging our confusion as to what we thought was happening to us. Our solace lay in knowing that we had at least together fallen into this abyss of strangeness. However, in our collective ignorance we were unsure as to how to proceed from that point on.

I am not suggesting that we were abandoned. To say this would be to minimize the role of our mothers' or guardians' input during the beginnings of the "big change." Their roles, however well intentioned, were incomplete rather than thorough. For as I said, one woman's outlook and her experiences are limited in defining fully this or any other major plateau. During this first pinnacle in woman's development, the cross-cultural rites of passage, in this case puberty, offered by women of experience would broaden understanding and support our psychological needs with a new-found confidence in the budding stage of womanhood.

Instead, we are often led to believe that this is either an unimportant or shameful period in our foundational development. Little attention or time is devoted to the first real celebration of the feminine principle coming to life within us. Right here, the damage is done.

For if from the get go this plateau is glossed over or minimized, then the beginnings of the knowledge of what womanhood really is fails to be instilled in the blossoming woman, for only ultimate realization over time creates ultimate potential. Without the rites of initiation and the learning that accompanies it, fertilization does not occur to strengthen the roots of the feminine principle. The end result is individual weakness or a partial bloom at full maturity.

In other words, if youth are left to free-fall through puberty and adolescence and these vulnerable teens are not rescued by concerned and selfless adults, then their inner self-esteem and outer positive body image will not be established. In its place lack of confidence and negative self-image will become the unstable roots that weaken all humanity.

Due to the latter already happening, we face growing problems with the youth. Children as young as twelve onwards are already on drugs. They are suffering from anxiety attacks, eating disorders, binge drinking, running away from home, promiscuity, losing themselves in rage and screamo music, and entertaining suicidal thoughts while inflicting self-mutilation upon themselves. Yes, there have always been forms of rebellion during the teen years, but no one can argue that these signs are not excessive and alarming. Just look at all the graffiti, property damage, break-ins and violence created by this unhappy group. Is the anger perhaps in part due to parental and societal neglect?

The antidote to everything gone sour is love in its many forms. With ongoing support, encouragement, understanding and caring, the adolescents would feel positive anticipation about growing up with less rage and self-destructive tendencies. This, of course, would not eliminate those many vulnerable moments of uncertainty that accompany teens as they journey through a strange land. That is normal for the revelations are important.

The preparatory period established by those in the know, for those who do not yet know, is a crucial stabilizer that in time moves us in the solid direction of beneficial outcomes. Thresholds are these preparatory periods and for everyone's sake, they need to be acknowledged fully and unconditionally supported by a society that remembers to care.

In earlier times, women's groups of the ancient ways looked upon the first plateau as a time for rejoicing. The threshold was celebrated with positive messages, teachings and fanfare that lasted for months until the group felt that the young initiate was prepared enough to begin the journey through adolescence.

Then why is it that what worked well was discarded? That

which proves itself as a positive should be left alone and left in place. Yet, humanity is noted to be its own worst enemy when it comes to an insatiable curiosity that is always altering and revising in the name of modernization. New ways are often weak and ineffective when compared to proven, old and sound traditions.

With new traditions called current lifestyles, we have lost the sensitivity of truly caring, to the point of indifference in some cases. As innate needs of interconnectedness are being consumed by attitudes of separateness, little concern is being given towards helping another. Welcome to the new and "improved" age of minimized involvement!

Our unsure teens need guidance by groups or circles in a position to offer assistance. Elders, both men and women, can provide the rituals of initiation as well as the guidelines that successfully lead us to manhood or womanhood. Teenagers are fast becoming lost souls due to lack of foundational footholds that would stabilize their unfoldment. Identity crises prevail as demonstrated by the hostile rebellions against members of society that no longer support youth fully during this first phase of their metamorphosis.

How is one expected to learn if not fully taught? What becomes of the apprentices if the masters, in their disinterest, no longer make themselves available? Not everything revolves around academic learning in sterile educational institutions. It is life that teaches about life. Those who have learned through life become the supporting teaching staff found outside of the classroom walls. In North America, the ritual of puberty is swept under the carpet. How does this unacknowledged event then create a sense of self-assuredness and pride in womanhood that a teen is becoming a part of?

One aspect of a woman's self-worth is her positive association with her newly formed physicality. It is one part of her entire being. Female sexuality is a part of her feminine force. It is during the impressionable period of her puberty that this is to be learned as she becomes comfortably acquainted with how her developed body works, her body rhythms and their connection to nature's cycles. If this is not encouraged giving her a healthy outlook she may in later years become ashamed of her body, hide it or even become abusive or neglectful towards it. Or she may become excessively pre-occupied with it as a sex symbol that solely identifies her, swallowing up the rest of who she truly is.

The trend of our ancestors is worth reviving. Apart from studying and applying past rituals and rites of passage in celebration, information should be gathered by those who will be the next generations' good-will teachers; by this I mean all types of information to psychologically and physically ease the transition. Here are some examples of topics:

forming one's individuality by investigating one's likes and dislikes, talents and skills, remaining independent in thought and not surrendering to peer pressure, information on healthy diet and herbal and vitamin supplementation to ease hormonal flux that creates heavy or painful periods, bloating, abdominal cramps and irritability, exercise and de-stressing methods to create a respectful relationship with our bodies. Depression or mood swings due to raging hormones have to be discussed by women who have experienced these symptoms and by health professionals offering their time to talk to groups of young women in puberty and in adolescence.

As well, it is during this particular passage that fertility should be celebrated as the special role women assume as repro-ducers of the race. Women's cycles that prepare us monthly for possible conception are not something we have to put up with as bothersome or a woman's curse. It is to be looked upon as a privilege to be able to create life in our wombs, the greatest miracle known to us on the earth plane. At this point we must emphasize that this fact alone makes woman a distinct and distinguished half of humanity. For it is only through woman that the essence of spirit is made flesh as a representative of the Divine Mother. The explanation of sex as also a vow of love would also be good to include at this time to encourage teens to value it and to give it the respect it is due.

Regarding woman's monthly cycles, I recently read an article that alarmed me. It talked of a new trend called period suppression methods for women who don't have the time to be inconvenienced by menstruation! This corporate-created, money-making pharmaceutical product totally going against nature's cycles reduces periods to three or four a year. As a backlash, it would serve us all right if humanity, in its stupidity, became totally sterile. Altering our normal cycles of womanhood will have dire effects in the future as we once again try to further disconnect from nature and the natural rhythm of our bodies.

Interesting that in the patriarchal society, once again woman is being encouraged to diminish her identity or alter it, while men on the other hand are being encouraged by the same pharmaceutical companies to augment their manhood by popping Viagra type pills to create eternal erections!

Womanhood is not something to be suppressed or ignored. It is not shameful or inconvenient. It is the ultimate expression of the feminine consciousness coursing through us and making itself known. Every attempt should be made to honor its arrival on a physical and psychological level. What better way than by older women welcoming young women into their circles of full femininity? Both informative and uplifting stories in women's groups should be continually shared as a part of collective women's experiences, to give re-assurance, a sense of optimism as well as enlightenment to those on the threshold of young womanhood.

We must hearten the spirit of the Goddess in each young woman and celebrate her in joyous anticipation as to what she will eventually contribute to the world as she unfolds confidently into fullness of being!

# 15

# The Climb: Threshold Two

Some behavioral therapists believe that certain plateaus are more important than others in our climb towards maturation. I do not. For each level sets the foundation to further build ourselves upon.

After experiencing the initial foundation of puberty that prepares us for adolescence, we eventually arrive at the second threshold. In olden times, it was referred to as the virgin/bride or maiden/bride passage. This implied the time when a young virgin woman, still living in her parents' house, ventured forth to become a wife. Today, women lose their virginity or move out long before the ring finds the finger. As well, many now choose common-law with male or same sex partners. Whatever the newest trend, what still remains as a challenge is the quality of that togetherness as it develops. The purpose of these unions is for that commitment to deepen over time. It appears, however, that the opposite is happening as divorce becomes common-place.

If before committing we could become somewhat more knowledgeable as to how to sow the seeds that will maintain a wholesome relationship, perhaps there would be less disappointment in love. Without a doubt, much of this wisdom needs to be learned as part of the pain of maturing emotionally and mentally, life being the great teacher/taskmaster responsible for this. However, much can also be taught by our elders as well.

Once again, this type of life knowledge is readily available in women's circles through their sharing of experiences and the invaluable insight and hindsight that comes with looking back upon challenges faced and conquered.

In adolescence onto our early twenties, exploring what it

means to be woman becomes a primary focus. We also begin to seek out our individual identity, detaching from our guardians in the process, for it is not parents that detach from their offspring; it is adolescents that step away. It is a healthy and a natural occurrence that enables the teen to begin to answer the question of "Who am I really?"

All cycles of growth eventually overflow into the next cycle and there comes a time, after self-exploration reeking with self-absorption, that the young adult desires to reconnect intimately and share their life with another. This innate need is to belong through bonding or mating. It is also triggered by the instinctual urge to procreate and preserve the species. Notice, I use the word reconnect and not attach, for the former is a healthy state while the other is not. To "wrap oneself around" or "live for" another is an unbalanced dependency that is not a sound union of two unique persons. On the flipside, excessive detachment in a committed relationship is no better for it signals issues of lack of trust in love.

As we arrive at the second gateway to the next frontier in our lives, we must begin at least, to learn the ground rules as to what "a healthy detached attachment" really means. A couple needs instruction separately and together about the delicate art of living together harmoniously, cherishing their chosen togetherness, while still retaining their identities. The loving personality nurtures. It does not control or dominate. This knowledge alone is basic information that can empower a relationship.

I am not suggesting that we can be taught to create a flawless union, for to begin with we are all somewhat flawed and we bring our goodness and our weaknesses with us wherever we go. However, we can be taught the basics that help establish a solid relationship that can survive the bumps in our personalities, simply by learning more about the art of loving.

In North American society, self-centeredness, indifference and intolerance are growing within us like malignant tumors.

Separateness consciousness promotes only self-love. There is no place in love for these destructive vices and they are better left outside of loving ties. We need to be aware of the basics that help expand love in a union so that it has a chance to survive from the start. We can also use some practical guidance to prepare us for what lies in store in the new life known as "the us." This togetherness brings its own set of challenges as we build a life together, which requires at times the surrender of the "I" needs for the good of the "us."

This type of preparatory work helps solidify the second foundation that we are getting ready to build the next segment of our lives upon. Equipped with other people's shared experiences and workable solutions, makes us more accomplished builders, which allows us to construct houses of brick rather than of straw.

The too little information I gathered about creating a lasting relationship was from observing one couple exclusively, my parents. As they stumbled along as husband and wife, not exactly the perfect models of harmonious union or experts in conflict resolution, their two children hid in the wings scribbling mental notes for later reference. My peers did exactly the same, for there was nowhere else to go to gather this information. No one or two people can demonstrate to us the vastness of love and its teachings.

Once again, as with the onset of puberty, we see the current trend. Those on this threshold as well are left to figure out everything as best they can. Experience might be one of our most reliable teachers, but impressionable people on a threshold do not have any experience. They must rely on others who have. Humans are complex in origin, therefore their needs are complex. Our learning and guidance have to be multidimensional and in depth, for unlike mammals, we function on more than instinctual responses. Where then are society's teachers of life knowledge?

The four plateaus of male and female maturation can be

likened to the four major levels of academia. One goes from preschool to elementary school on to high school and lastly to university, college or trade school. In each level one finds a bevy of teachers, teachers' aides, principals, department heads, guidance counselors, academic advisors, security staff, schoolyard monitors, nurses, volunteers and administrators. This slew of people not only offers support and direction, they also ease the transitions from one scholastic level to the next.

I find it rather naive of modern societies to prioritize by creating endless ultra-efficient facilities for those who pursue book knowledge, and neglect facilities for enhancing personal development and the teaching of both social and life skills. This area of learning is simply not recognized, funded or developed to meet the needs of the people. In past history of various civilizations, women attended to these needs of their communities. One such need was to prepare upcoming maiden/brides for coupledom. It was a gift or dowry offered by the village women, filled with jewels of wisdom and priceless, practical skills.

Today, women venture forth knowing plenty about sex, little about love and even less about practical household skills. Young men appear not to know much either. While the governments sleep, let the women do as they did before. Councils of women can position themselves in their communities and take on the teachings and preparatory work that focuses on facilitating this and the other three major transitional periods in a woman's life. Men can do the same through brotherhoods.

For example, in anticipation of the maiden/bride period being ushered in topics of discussion may include: skills as a homemaker, balancing work and home responsibilities, integrating the mate's family into your life, the art of effective communication between couples, retaining individuality in unity, equality in relationship, establishing shared responsibilities, respecting the unique identity of one's spouse, and so on.

Apart from planned partnership with its practical considerations, there is another area that needs addressing. I touched upon this earlier. It is knowledge on the art of loving. What is selflessness, sacrifice, compromise, cooperation, forgiveness, loyalty, honesty, respect and acceptance? These are a few of the building blocks that form all types of wholesome relationships and these virtues, dormant in young adults, need to be awakened. To first understand, then finally accept these as uncompromising truths and then to apply them in our lives takes time, years in fact. The earlier this instruction is commenced the quicker the results attained.

Wouldn't it be nice to put most divorce lawyers out of business!

Coaching is much easier done in a group setting. By this, I mean informed groups or circles teaching apprentice groups. This way offers a multitude of experiences and points of view to broaden the scope of learning in its well-roundedness.

Call me redundant, but I cannot help stress enough how important it is for women to take care of each other, especially during our vulnerable states on a threshold. We can thus emerge more thoroughly informed as to who we truly are capable of becoming and what we can achieve when we are somewhat prepared. Perhaps this "way of woman" reborn can, in time, strengthen the fragile state of womanity.

We need to re-ignite the group consciousness mentality found in hubs of women of the past that helped produce more stable societies. Eventually, these village groups moved into the church setting, as it became the heart of the community. Today's cities and municipalities are becoming vast and many churches are closing their doors. However, communities still retain their smallness. Women's circles as part of community services, charitable or not, can fill the void that has been created by the disappearances of churches and small villages, but first we must realize that something is missing.

Let us not forget that collective consciousness produces a

balanced interdependence that allows for a tight netting to support and ease the internal struggles of the human psyche. People have little place left to turn to for assistance except perhaps to the therapist's couch which is often as expensive as visiting a lawyer's office. Services offered by openhearted sororities and fraternities as helping hands, should not only be everywhere but should be free to their community residents.

Arrival at the threshold of puberty is not less challenging than arriving at the maiden/bride pinnacle that leads to yet further life challenges. This second threshold needs as much concerned attention as did the first and the next awaiting threshold, that of motherhood.

# 16

# The Climb: Threshold Three

Everything in nature, ourselves included, is destined to come into its maturity, fruition or blossoming. If nature has her way and we don't impede this growth we will certainly arrive. If however, we willfully resist, choose to remain ignorant, impose upon ourselves negative, self-limiting thinking or are not motivated, we arrest our growth. Instead we prematurely start to decay psychologically and physically. It's a do-or-die situation. Each plateau is of paramount importance and each threshold must be integrated successfully to push us forward confidently.

A woman's inner destiny is to radiate her inner virtues of the heart and her soulfulness. How she does it is left to personal choice and is her outer destiny.

The third plateau brings us to motherhood itself. Preparing to make that decision of committing to it or not is the third threshold. Inside every woman, barren or not, lies the cosmic mother. Naturally and instinctively, we can at any moment slip into this role. Mothering is first associated with the rearing of children, but we can mother in many other ways in the world, even if we do not have children of our own. I will expand upon this in the section entitled "Childless Nurturer."

In the past we succumbed to social pressures to have children simply because a married woman was expected to raise a family, sometimes bearing fourteen children in her lifetime. Boy, am I glad those days are gone! To have children now has become a choice of free will. It is an inner prompting to push us to develop further our loving capacities by experiencing selflessness through nurturing.

Our instinctual drives, on the other hand, prior to peri-menopause ensure the continual procreation of our species.

Plateau two, with its impulses to find a suitable mate is the precursor to plateau three with its urges to parent. The stability of solid love found between mates nurtures and provides, in part, a safe haven for a growing child's psyche and body. Establishing a loving relationship between mates is therefore a first priority. Accidentally getting pregnant before we are stable in our relationship with our partner is a poor beginning for the child-to-be. It is therefore necessary to work with women before they conceive and are still in the planning stage, to ensure that there is a real readiness between spouses before a family is started.

Let's connect back to nature. The bird does not lay her eggs until she and her partner have fully prepared the nest. Mammals first find and then prepare an abode before bringing their offspring into the world. We, with our intelligence, should be doing the same. I am not referring here to just getting the baby's room ready.

A woman contemplating a first pregnancy needs to address a list of possible developments to limit stressful consequences that could affect her, her mate and the newborn. One reason being is that young children do not have well developed coping skills. They absorb the happenings in their environment through their feelings alone. Negative feelings from their surroundings instill fear, nervousness and anxiety which can manifest in ongoing illnesses and feelings of insecurity that they will carry into adulthood. Unresolved, they create chronic stress that will express itself in many ways throughout their lifetimes.

To minimize this, parents-to-be need lengthy counseling on parenthood, just as a young woman needs help in preparation for motherhood by those who have passed through the mothering phase.

Issues that the young woman needs to look closely at are plentiful. Some include: What normal physical changes can a pregnant woman expect? What potential complications can they in preparedness, prevent? What psychological mood shifts will occur with hormonal surges? What is postpartum depression? What dietary considerations, herbal aids, exercise, natural vitamins and natural therapies are good when carrying a child?

Are we prepared, without question, to love our distorted and bloated body that will be us in our third trimester? Are we ready to accept that as our body becomes more uncomfortable that intimacy with our partner might be compromised? What are alternatives to keep the love flowing with our partner? Are we aware that negative thoughts, bouts of depression and anxiety, as well as an unsettled environment can physically impair the fetus? Are we aware that soothing music, meditation, relaxation techniques and nature walks activate our feel good hormones, which enhance the growth of the fetus? How do we naturally minimize heartburn, swelling, constipation and all those joyless side effects of later pregnancy?

What type of practical skills do we need to ready ourselves for a newborn and then a toddler? What do we need to know about breastfeeding (for example eating food from the cabbage family gives the baby gas and cramps!). Are we ready to accept the fact that no matter how doting a daddy might be, it is the mother that the child first strongly bonds with and therefore it is the female that is the primary caregiver to her child? Knowing this are we capable of accepting this long-term intrusion that will crowd us out of our own private space without regret or resentment?

Are we ready to sacrifice and become selfless? Are we having children for the right reasons? Are both parents truly on board with this decision? How will our lifestyles change? Are we financially prepared? Do we have unrealistic expectations that our mother, mother-in-law or the daycare will step in to raise our children for us? Do we realize what an honor and a privilege it is to be able to birth or adopt a child as a representation of the Universal Mother? Finally, what does it mean to be the ultimate nurturer and creator of life?

A semblance of preparation will serve as an invaluable reference guide when we are immersed in the thick of things. Don't expect your doctor to put the time aside to delve into the answers and concerns of the above questions. So I fall back upon women's circles to be able to provide the schooling in this area, balanced with a sprinkling of ritual and rites of passage to celebrate this wonderful opportunity to create and nurture a new life and capture Divine spirit in the womb.

The decision to venture forth should come from an informed choice, not from impulsiveness or by accident. I see all around me the sad cases of damaged children growing into damaged teenagers. I cannot help, through an innate knowing, to attribute this often to inadequate parenting caused by those who entered parenthood ill-prepared or with absence of thought. The end result is really messed up kids.

We simply owe it to our children to ready ourselves as much as possible to be able to provide them with a secure home life, psychological stability, and an endless outpouring of love. Otherwise, we are doing a poor job and this is not an option. Parenting, especially mothering, is by far the most important job on the planet and one should realize this before attempting it half-heartedly or avoid it altogether, if that will be the case, for the sake of the children! Good parenting requires the full energy and dedication of two devoted parents who have tried to prepare themselves to the best of their ability.

I speak now as a mother. Nurturer is the first role of womanity, her highest priority. The selfless, dedicated bonding with her children is the deepest, purest and most satisfying loving experience she will ever have. It is the perfect antidote for self-centeredness and the unexpected reward is that when we love in this way, it returns back to us tenfold, somehow.

# 17

# The Climb: Threshold Four

The doorway of the fourth threshold is that of peri-menopause, defined as the beginning of hormonal changes that lead us into menopause. Usually this occurs between our mid forties to late fifties. In certain European cultures, age fifty-five is heralded as the official arrival of crone-hood, or the final plateau. In actuality it is the time of birthing of total woman now infinitely wise and in this wisdom empowered. It is an honorable position of knowing, as both life knowledge and inner wisdom have broadened and deepened. Add to this her well-honed intuition and she is on the final threshold leading into completeness.

At least this is the way it should be if woman lived in a world that did not repress her growth towards self-actualization. She should now arrive at that place where she reveres herself as wise woman, and is respected Matriarch due to a life lived long. However, the modern outlook of patriarchal prejudice against women, especially the aging female, has deflated this glorious period and stripped her of her worth, with the false image that senior women are rather insignificant and useless. No longer acknowledged by a male dominant society due to her loss of sexual appeal, or physical desirability, she is left by the side of life's road to decay.

The irony in all of this is if she listens to her heightened wisdom, and has broken free from the chains that have kept her captive in a man's world, she will not buy into this shallow stupidity. She realizes, as total woman, that she no longer needs validation from anyone to appreciate her own worth; she has arrived at powerful realizations and in so doing has transcended her one dimensional physical sexuality. In its place she embraces her inner femininity which becomes her new, multi-dimensional sexual identity. For she is now spiritually, emotionally, and mentally, the embodiment of wisdom and wholeness.

Yet, the final threshold leading into this period of total womanness does not find most women in a state of eager anticipation to being so close to a contented state of maturity. Instead, we find them too often depressed, insecure, confused and vulnerable. They, as a product of society's male-sided views, are convinced that youthfulness was the golden season of their lives and aging only brings with it decline and decrepitude. With brave faces some do indeed fool the world, but most are inwardly convinced that it is all downhill from here on having been brainwashed to accept this.

This threshold can therefore be two-faced. For those who come from woman's inner wisdom and from encouragement from peers, this plateau is a wonderful time in their lives. For others, who insist on feeling "passé", they start losing motivation and direction. If they are unable to graciously let go of what was, accept what now is, and use what it takes to create new beginnings for what can be, then they have resigned themselves to simply tread the waters of life with no movement forward in their future. "The only thing constant is change." People need constantly to change for the better as a part of innate programming that pushes us to evolve and become the best we possibly can be, no matter our age. This ongoing inner process either slightly or significantly transforms our outer life.

We see, especially in the older generation of seniors, that many entertain thoughts that keep them fixed and they are referred to as obstinate, inflexible or set in their ways. Underlying this behavior is often the fear of change or just a comfortable lull of inertia. This results in stagnation and premature decay.

Fertilization, gestation, birth, unfoldment, death, decay and rebirth are the perpetual universal cycles. These continually repeat themselves within us as mini-cycles propelling us forward, sometimes against our will, towards life's ongoing new experiences that we can only benefit from as personal growth challenges.

Interestingly enough, we are not hesitant in youth to forge ahead and make subtle and dramatic changes right until we enter our late fifties. Why then, do many of us become immovable after that age? To slow down and pace ourselves is understandable, but to settle into the rut of sameness, day in and day out, sucks the enthusiasm out of our life and is a tragedy as the once living begin to become the living dead.

People who digress into rigidity often develop miserable personalities that can be referred to as the sour grapes persona infecting those around them. They resist, for whatever reason, to move forward and be flexible with new possibilities that feed their need for continual growth and appease their curiosities. We age rapidly when we are fixated only on being old.

I once read an excerpt in an oriental philosophy, whose source evades me:

"Be like the shoots of the mighty bamboo, well rooted yet flexible, moving every which way with the winds of life."

Not so very long ago, maturity offered woman the throne of the tribal matriarch or clan matriarch. As the eldest woman, the crone was worshipped for her wisdom. She was the revealer of great truths. She passed on ancient traditions, teachings and ways to live. This is her earned place in society and she should still be the center of attention, busy passing on her traditions and wisdom. Today the senior matriarch is unjustly demeaned as a withering old woman and is treated courteously out of a sense of pity rather than out of respect. Women innately know that crone wisdom deserves to be revered not ignored, elevated not suppressed. Yet, neglecting her runs rampant. In a man's world, fascinated by youthfulness and sex appeal, older women struggle. But must they continue to do so? It is precisely at this stage in our womanhood that it should be all coming together and the power behind self-acceptance and self-love actualized.

When we re-unite in women's circles this power of self-confidence surges, for collectiveness provides the milieu that helps create the assured self. If not before, then during the second half of life women should find one another once more and hang on tightly to these sisterhoods. Coming together in groups helps dispel feelings of social isolation and with it the accompanying feelings of neglect.

The period through our fifties and onwards is referred to metaphysically as the butterfly period. The final metamorphosis as the chrysalis of limitations finally breaks apart and permits us to soar. A time of liberation, de-cluttering our lives of the "have-tos" and "shoulds" of others' expectations. As heavy responsibilities and our illusions drop away, there is new-found freedom. It is about arriving. It is not about prematurely withering away. In crone-hood, if not before, it is intended for us to finally acknowledge our collective interconnectedness as well as to express the glorious unique self that makes us individually special.

The second half of life or plateau four, is all about "me time" indulgence. Crone-hood intensifies the need to complete the journey back to ourselves, to honor ourselves. This period is the final gift of time set aside by the universe for full soul expression. That part of you that has yearned to live your life as you've always wanted to, to fulfill the destiny of your specialness without selfish motive or harmful intent. These are one's soul dreams, unfulfilled passions or deep needs that want to finally lead us to the pinnacle of our life, the completion of our destiny.

The moon Goddess Diana represents empowerment and self-assurance for the older woman choosing to live in accordance with the Divine Feminine within her. In this connection is her solidness of being. Through that confidence she finds her liberation to bring forth the possibilities within her, to create herself fully once and for all.

Finally, the now developed trinity of the whole woman, that of innocence, maturity and elder wisdom should make her invincible even if the physical self is beginning to wane. It is the pursuit of fully opening our thousand petalled lotus that one should now be focused upon. Crone-hood is a fertile time of self-creation, if you allow your intuitive impulses and soul urges to guide you towards your blossoming. As your body begins its hormonal changes, let your soul begin to flow outwards. It will inspire you.

When we start saying that "we are now too old" or "that ship has sailed" we are dousing our own inner flame. The majority of us, at this stage, have not yet arrived at that place of fulfillment that comes from the soul's needs attained or from connection to our roots in the collective feminine. Most of us are still journeying, many have become lost woman. In our mid-life confusion, teetering on the step that leads us onto the last plateau, we need clarity of purpose.

I can confidently say that a good place to become re-motivated is in the company of women in the same stage of life or older who are wise enough to be expressing who they truly are. Women are not solitary birds, they fly in flocks. In their natural ways of networking, they can re-invent each other. By this I mean directing the lost woman back to her true identity by encouraging her to acknowledge her deep, unfulfilled desires and needs.

Women helping women keep us focused on finding our way back to who we were once becoming way back when, before life broadsided us with responsibilities and societal expectations. As we obliged, not knowing any better, we began to lose more and more of ourselves. Our hopes, dreams and aspirations that were to create ourselves and our lives were shelved. Few had the smarts in youth to stay the course remaining loyal to their true identities that were developing. Youth may be filled with vitality but it is also filled with naivety. We are not learned enough at that tender stage of life to follow our own star. We, therefore, end up following the herd of drones into a mundane existence. Accumulated wisdom and life knowledge manages eventually to switch on a light bulb so we can once again see that we are heading in a direction that in the long run will not satisfy an inner gnawing. Over fifty is an opportunity to leave the herd of aimlessly, wandering discontents behind.

Peri-menopause and onwards is misinterpreted in modern cultures as a negative experience due to loss of youthfulness. The body may start to wane, but wisdom keeps expanding and through its own vitality re-ignites and re-energizes us. So, not much is really lost as we age, rather much is gained.

Women coming together help magnify these realizations by creating ongoing celebrations for this final life stage. Socializing, laughing and creating together in group settings is a natural extension of the collective feminine we spoke of earlier.

Topics in such circles that would uplift us on this final frontier may include menopause as a time of arrival, researching the history of the crone and her powers, living our passions and dreams, the dimensions of whole woman, aging gracefully through a positive attitude, maintaining a healthy lifestyle, liberating the soul self, how to remain active and connected to society, changing careers in crone-hood, developing more fully our gifts and talents, dealing with thoughts of mortality and immortality, letting go of mothering responsibilities, how to enjoy a more leisurely life, involving oneself more in community work and projects that give us joy, exploring our feminine spirituality and so forth.

It takes time and dedication to shift and move in a new direction, in this case back towards the "me." We must remember that in the beginning we started off only with the "me." "Me" entered into various types of partnerships over a lifetime and lost itself to "us" relationships, personally and in our careers. "Me" is still very much there waiting to be recognized and liberated from all those "us" attachments as a way of developing the collective and the unique self.

We can easily reclaim it and celebrate it once more. For it is "me" that one entered this life with and it is only "me" that one will leave with. "Me" needs to attain its maturity of purpose through full expression of itself by propelling its identity into an awaiting world.

There is a profound saying that sums up what I am trying to bring across to you on the final threshold:

"And just when the caterpillar resigned itself to its perceptions that life would soon be over, it became a butterfly!"

# SECTION TWO

# 1

# Woman of the Earth, Hearth and Heart

In part, the tremendous force of collective consciousness found in woman, is defined by deep intuition, passionate creativity, infinite love and ageless wisdom. Woman expresses these qualities primarily through home life, the heart self and in her affiliation with Mother Earth. As she now becomes severed from her soul messages and uprooted from traditions based upon the ancient mysteries of the Goddess culture, she joins the endangered list, not physically but internally.

In this part of the book I look more closely at the properties of Chart A focusing on the female's primary roles as nurturer, imparter of spiritual truths, nature healer and creative creator. Woman of the earth, hearth and heart best define her on this plane of existence and as we once again identify with and revive this deepest nature, the sacred Feminine is released from bondage.

Referring to Chart A, we see that women's properties fit under the headings of earth-oriented, family inclined and heart inspired. The exceptions being those of her as contractive, associated with the negative pole and connected to the circular or cyclical cycles. These three, refer to universal patterns exclusively. There are many more, of course, that we need not be concerned about. I have included these three as samples to show the reader how vast the properties of the feminine principle are in the cosmos. For example, the universe goes in cycles where it is in a state of expansion and then in contraction. This is represented to us in such examples as the natural occurring movements of the moon, sun, earth and stars. Just look at the moon's contractive light crescent and then at the expansive light of the full moon. Observe the rising up and receding tidal swells of incoming and outgoing tides. We find in summer the expansiveness of heat and in winter the contractiveness of cold. Bringing it closer to ourselves, our continual breathing is also a part of the universal rhythm of expansion and contraction, which is also found in the heartbeat. Every organism in the universe is either expanding or contracting at any given moment in time. The feminine pole represents the movement of contraction.

As for the negative pole being a part of the feminine, it is only once again about us being a part of all that is. Negative charge is one half of chemical and electro-magnetic properties of the cosmos, so is positive charge which exudes from the male polarity. The North and South Poles of earth are two examples of magnetism. The earth's atmosphere is saturated with positive and negative air ions. Excessive positive ions, through studies, appear to have an unhealthy effect on the human body and our frame of mind. Negative ions have a healthy effect.

Females are of the negative pole and are therefore highly responsive to the healing powers of negative ions, while males are much less so. While scientists scratch their heads about this, it makes perfect sense to the esoteric student knowing the cosmic properties of the woman. Negative ions are generally produced by radioactive rays in the atmosphere, through ongoing photo synthesis of plants, and through bodies of water and any moisture. Mother Earth is eighty per cent water exuding mostly negative ions, like a woman!

It is little wonder that after the rain falls, the water molecules in the air, filled with negative ions, refresh and make us feel good. People feel the same near any clean body of water, like swimming in lakes, sitting by trickling brooks and waterfalls, and standing alongside the ocean shore.

Excessive positive ions are produced in such places as the air prior to storms, in strong winds, in stagnant heat and in areas of concentrated air pollution. No wonder city slickers are so testy and irritable! If excessive positive ions have detrimental effects on us, we can see from this reality alone that climate change is going to bring serious problems to our physical and psychological health. The storms and winds are increasing, the temperature is inching up, pollution is thick, and the destruction of greenery is ruthless. In a man's world nature is an afterthought. In a true woman's world it is a forethought.

In the name of making money, technology is inventing apparatuses that produce negative ions to feed our malnourished well-being. For example, infra red lamps, heating pads and saunas with their negative charge output relieve pain, reduce inflammation and re-energize us. Or we can save our money and just go out into nature.

After such artificial treatments we plunk ourselves in front of TVs, computer monitors and cell phones to name a few. This cancels out everything. For these inventions of a techno age gone crazy produce a bombardment of positive ion energy. Positive ions lower our resistance and devitalize us. Again, we could find more "natural" past times. It is also positive ions that create acid solutions in a base. Acid rain, as a result of air pollution, which is of positive charge, is poisoning the planet's body as well as our own. It is going to take more than the elimination of plastic grocery bags or munching on raw vegetables to reverse the damage that is causing the planet to die and is making our bodies sicker with each passing day.

All life, including the planet, is surrounded by magnetism created by the balance of positive and negative charge. This is called electro-magnetic fields or, as a clairvoyant mystic prefers, auras. Balance is the re-occurring word associated with universal intention. As it sits now, in a male empowered world that discredits women, there are heartless actions towards the earth mother that are creating excessive positive ions in the atmosphere. This is a major factor in the upheavals in our climate. Indifference is not a part of collective feminine wisdom. For this reason alone women need to defend the negative charge of nature which enhances their own personal negative charge.

Let us now move onto another trait of the Feminine Divine. Woman is associated with that which is circular or cyclical if you prefer. This aspect refers to the geometry of creation found in arcs, cones, spirals and circles, but not in linear patterns such as lines and angles associated with the masculine principle. Those who are linear minded, or of male, left-brain thought, believe the Universe to be moving forward. They believe that it has boundaries and is therefore finite. Those of the feminine thought persuasion believe it to be curved and infinite. Due to the fact that opposite polarities work together to create the whole, my guess is that both theories are somehow correct.

Having now touched upon properties of circular, negative and contractive to make clearer their association with the feminine force on a vaster level, we can return to discussing earth woman and the traits that design her, once again referring to Chart A.

As with all mammals, man and woman love in their own ways. I believe that at this point in our evolution it is woman that possesses the power of transformative love that can heal and unite. Men seem to struggle more with demonstrating love and openly displaying sensitivity and empathy. Maybe it is not so much that they cannot or will not, perhaps it is simply that they are not equipped to do so, as per investigation of Chart B. If the dormant, feminine principle in males is awake then this is not necessarily the case. Even so, it is always so much easier for woman to assume this role since she is comfortable with her emotions and often thinks with her heart. There is a cute little quip I insert here: "Men are like mascara. At the first sign of emotions, they begin to run."

For the most part it is woman that is open to her profound feelings and intuition and accesses them rather easily if she has not been falsely programmed to do otherwise. When in a balanced state, *true* woman is able to conjure up the loving energy that connects heart to heart and enhances deep seated collective consciousness or unity mindedness.

Examining Chart A once more, we see the traits of benevolence, tolerance, sensitivity, passivity, nurturance, intuitiveness, responsiveness, discreetness, flexibility, yielding, tenderness, sensuality and that of peacemaker. All of these indicate that woman has what it takes to be a true vehicle of love.

Now you might say, "Wait a minute here, I know plenty of women who possess little if any of these traits." Point acknowledged! My response is that we are all somewhat damaged. Some much more than others and due to this we have adapted into untrue versions of the authentic woman. Those who have been more seriously injured by life situations have closed off many parts of their beautiful potential and have become instead, insensitive, abrasive, nasty, self-centered and so on. They have not morphed into men in this case but have become weaker examples of the feminine principle.

There are numerous reasons as to why this could have happened, I list but a few. Perhaps their negative environment initiated internal changes that re-programmed them to be able to survive, fit in, or to tolerate unloving or harsh conditions in their formative years. Others role modeled after their own mothers who were, perhaps, the initial damaged ones. Others had no mother and mimicked their fathers' behavior or were brought up with no sisters just a house full of brothers.

Some traits, or lack of, are learned. In some cultures women are taught to be excessively passive, introverted and painfully submissive. In others they are encouraged to be tough, unemotional and aggressive. Whatever the case, it is all about inappropriate programming that produces an end result. Keep in mind your own interpretations and their accuracy. For example, a woman that doles out tough love at times may appear to be a hard woman especially if it is directed your way. This is an example of the other side of woman discussed earlier. It is not to be confused with one who has become a hardened woman or unnatural woman.

It is true that woman of the highest feminine consciousness is a rarity for she exhibits all of Chart A's qualities. Damaged as all of us are we can still strive for that excellence, once we have a blueprint to use as our guideline. There are over fifty virtues alone that define the composition of the loving nurturer. They include: kindness, generosity, selflessness, humbleness, caring, compassion, forgiveness, reliability, acceptance, mercy, gentleness, respectfulness, thoughtfulness, helpfulness and consideration. I don't know about you, but I am still very much a work in progress!

Woman of the hearth is an extension of woman of the heart as she expands herself into selfless service for her family and extended family. My twenty-seven year old son once explained to me the reason he felt he turned out all right and stable. He attributed this to the fact that I was always in the home when he returned from school and was ready to listen to his stories. He told me this constancy developed a sense of security that he could build a solid, assured self upon. In other words, love could always be found in the same place and was available at all times.

I mentioned earlier on that a natural element for woman is her home base, whether she lives alone, with a mate, or with oodles of children like the woman who, in the rhyme, lived in a shoe. She has a driving nesting instinct. She needs to feather a nest and fill it with what gives her identity and comfort. It is her sanctuary, her ongoing creative expression of self, her hub for family togetherness, her social headquarters, her hideaway, her sacred space and her palace even if it is a humble abode.

On the other hand, most men who live alone simply occupy these square boxes of various sizes. In it are found the essentials, a toothbrush in the bathroom, a liter of milk in the fridge and an unmade bed. Usually their abode is void of plant life, pets, or other life forms that would enhance the energy of their box. It is simply a place to sleep, shower and drink that liter of milk, probably expired. Even the affluent, single man's mansion feels incomplete. It lacks the heartbeat of a woman's presence or even his presence. Single men rarely linger at home.

The heart fires of a woman are the hearth fires that transform a house into a home that invites one to stay for a while. Without her, or without her committing her time and energy to it, it simply remains a square box crammed with furnishings yet still somehow exuding a feeling of vast emptiness.

Then there is woman of the earth. Who is she and why do we conclude that she has this attachment to nature? It has a lot to do with her ability to work with and sense the energies of nature, a little bit like animals sensing weather patterns well before any changes occur. Woman is the gatherer, but first she needs her harvest. She has the "touch" for planting and growing vegetables, fruits, flowers, herbs and anything else she puts her mind to. She also has the knack of turning the produce into nourishing meals. She knows when to pick her herbs, which ones to avoid, and which to mix into foods. She is also adept at preserving, canning, pickling and drying her bounty that she has raised from seed.

As she adorns the outside of her home with annuals, perennials and vegetation she enthuses over, she somehow knows, or used to know their properties. She knew which parts of the flowers to eat, what roots and leaves could make teas, which plant life was to be used for medicinal purposes, and which were strictly decorative. If each woman would return to this inner connection filling her lawn or balcony with herbs and gardens and the inside of her home with the soothing beauty of plant life, we would all benefit from the abundance bursting forth. Imagine the increase in negative ions as well!

As a healer, there was a time when she used only natural compounds found in nature's pharmacy to make poultices, compresses, expectorants, salves, ointments and brews. Woman was intuitive doctor in her family as part of her gifts as nurturer. The overcrowding of hospitals is partly due to the fact that medicine woman of the family is virtually extinct. In less than seventy-five years she has become ignorant in this area, barren of her healing powers.

So true woman exudes nature. Urban woman is so disconnected that she is alien to this part of herself. True woman connects to Earth Mother's rhythms and moods. She communes with and befriends Gaia through rituals that allow her to honor the seasons, the cycles, the solstices and equinoxes, the harvest, the sun and moon, the water, trees, plants, wildlife, the rains and even the air we breathe. These are her ways, ancient traditions lost to the city slicker. Modernized woman will sadly just keep getting further away from Earth Mother as expanding cities destroy Gaia's fertility and abundance.

Dr. David Suzuki, famous international environmentalist for nearly fifty years, spoke recently in Montreal, Quebec, one of his many stops in Canada. He loudly declared that even after fifty years of devoting his energies, alongside other environmentalists, to raising consciousness in the public, he feels that he and his colleagues have failed. He went on to say that our highest priority of the self and of governments has become our jobs, and little else matters. We refuse in our selfishness to become ecologically considerate. He warns us that if we do not shift our priorities from personal comforts and acquisitions we will be doomed, for we choose, without conscience, to violate nature. Now to enhance the work begun by these environmentalists it is women who need to take a powerful stance to protect the planet, as the keeper of nature's mysteries that help define the female consciousness. I mentioned earlier on that negative ions are created by vegetation and that woman is also of negative charge. This, in itself, brings home the point that woman is the gatekeeper for nature, for it enhances her makeup. There is definitely a connection here.

There is no use denying all that woman is. We cannot change that which is unchangeable. Why would we want to? Why would we want to avoid being our true selves? We should honor it and let our womanhood excel by totally expressing it. It is only through self-discovery or the raising of her consciousness that woman becomes aware of the Divine Feminine blueprint coursing through every energy line of her mental, emotional, spiritual and physical beingness.

Regarding women as the knights that serve Gaia, it is high time that we realize that Gaia is a representation of what we are all becoming. She mirrors the symptoms of a diseased, toxic, weakened and distressed humanity. As a woman, Gaia is not taken seriously in a man's world. Woman should intuitively know better for they are so connected to Her They are the ones that should be taking action, en masse if need be, to push for total environmental protection. As a side note, one country is standing up for this great lady. In 2008 Bolivia distributed a pamphlet to the United Nations listing the 10 commandments that were set by it to save the planet. One was to eliminate capitalism! Bolivia tabled a draft at the U.N. proposing a treaty giving Mother Earth the same rights as humans, preventing insensitive corporations from exploiting, dominating and destroying what is Hers. I keep my fingers crossed that this new trend will have great impact one day.

Gaia is more powerful than all of us put together. She does not need us but we desperately need her. In the end she will heal herself, this is the good news. The sad news is that if apathy amongst her female warriors continues, humanity will pay dearly as Gaia rights the wrongs unaided in order to ensure her survival.

# 2

# Maternal Instincts

They say that to look into the face of a doting mother is to look into the face of the Goddess within the God.

The virtues I listed in the previous chapter that make up a loving being are always of seven levels of attainment according to spiritual laws of unfoldment. Our inner programming is to raise ourselves up to the highest level of each virtue in the seven-fold journey towards highest consciousness. I present the following fable as an example:

There was once a person who climbed the mountain to speak with the wise one. The visitor asked what they should do about a persistent problem. The sage suggested that the visitor go back down to the village and live through the virtue of kindness. This they did, but the problem remained. Up the mountain, a second time, the person went to complain. The wise one responded with, "My child, return once more to your village and be kinder still." They did, things improved but not enough. The third, fourth, fifth and sixth visits brought the same advice. The seventh time the all knowing one said, "You are making great progress. Go back one more time and become, even more so, the kindest person you know you can be. Then live at this highest level for the rest of your days."

Kindness is but one of over fifty such virtues we must tackle to reach where we are destined to arrive one day. How many lifetimes will this seven-fold journey take! If not here then somewhere else in our travels in the infinite galaxy.

A *true* mother magnifies to some level these virtues. She is as close as we come to seeing the exaltation of love in a mere human displayed. A nurturing mother always puts her children at the centre of her world even after they have reached adolescence and beyond. There appears to be no sacrifice that is too great for her when it comes to giving from the heart. It is amazing how a wonderful mother's love is inexhaustible. She might not encompass all the virtues but her love is unconditional with the purest intent nonetheless. Until we all evolve, a true mother is the best example humanity has as its model when it comes to selfless love.

She is a reminder of what a person is capable of becoming when devoted to the well-being of others. When we love so purely we have no expectations of reward or even acknowledgement. This is the highest achievement one can attain. What a splendid world we would live in if all of us would aspire to this level of caring. Mothers create their offspring not only in their wombs. They mould them into the adults they will become one day based on the amount of affection they give, their moral and spiritual teachings as well as the example they set.

For love begets love. Love heals. Love nourishes the soul of others. Love protects. Love is forgiving. Love is stable and reliable. Love gives comfort. Love encourages and supports. Love is infinitely patient. Love empowers others. Love opens the heart of another. Love transforms. Love is non-restrictive nor possessive. Love is limitless in its possibilities. Love creates only beauty and harmony.

A heavy load for any mother to aspire to. To be so caring and self-less is the ultimate service to others. We are all born to mothers. We are all supposed to be given this beautiful beginning just by being received immediately into the heart of the mother that births us. It is set up that way as an extension of Divine love as the Universe hands an incarnating soul into the hands of a welcoming mother. Yet, it is often not this way, for many a sad reason due to human limitations, selfishness, ignorance, personal baggage and circumstance. Mothers are capable of giving all that I mentioned if they take their role seriously and value its importance. Within themselves they have been equipped to do so. If they can excel as nurturers, their children too will excel as valuable, solid citizens of society.

It seems that children are born into a tiny bubble to snugly contain them while in their innocence until they have been readied to face the world. Once that bubble bursts because they have outgrown it, they are thrust into reality equipped only with the sword and shield formed from a mother's imparted wisdom and her protective love. Would we want to provide anything less for our beloved children?

We, as mothers, can only remind ourselves to keep striving for excellence, not for perfection, for within us all lie imperfections that we taint our children with unintentionally. With each successive generation we all evolve. In so doing we work out some of these inherited glitches so as to one day reach the goal of becoming beings of pure love through enlightenment. Mothering, as heart of the family, is a full time commitment. There are no acceptable shortcuts and little resting time. It is a choice though. Not every woman decides to be a child bearer. However, once the choice to mother has been made, the sacrifice needed is non-negotiable. I cannot stress this point loud enough!

Half-hearted parenting, part-time parenting or irresponsible parenting are not options. Lack of adequate nurturing is inexcusable. That which is neglected does not thrive. A love starved child becomes a weakened, damaged adult. Women have it within them to instinctively and intuitively nurture. It is their prize ability. The intent is the most important ingredient. Yet, in today's world of mislaid priorities, mothers replace themselves with day cares, nannies and the empty house that does the babysitting for the absentee mother. Do not contemplate motherhood if this will be the case.

In the words of Strickland Gillilan, deceased American poet:

"You may have tangible wealth untold, caskets of jewels and coffers of gold. Richer than I can ever be – but I had a mother who read to me."

Remember my story of my son. Out of the mouths of babes comes the piercing truth. As creators, we create that which we set our minds to. Dedication rewards the devotee. Good is adequate, better, an improvement, and being our best the most honorable achievement.

Mothers make or break their children. The child gravitates towards her first for all their needs. It is instinctual. If she is unavailable, the child adapts and latches on to the father or the person that is most constant in their lives. Dads can be great but they are not equipped to be moms; properties in their polarity (Chart B) verify this. They too can be loving, protectors and providers, but nurturing is a skill that is weak in them. This is because they tend to be rational, logical and practical.

All children are flawed for they are only human. We are all born with limitations or weaknesses either physically, emotionally or mentally. This is each person's karma, so to speak. Even perfect parenting, if it was possible, could not erase the trouble spots found in little humans. We do the best we can with what we have to work with and not blame ourselves or our children in the end. We simply love the child for the child.

However, when I see children that are psychologically damaged, under stress, acting out, troublemakers, bullies, belligerent, introverted, filled with fears and insecurities, are unhappy, depressed, timid or sad little ones, I cannot help but look right at their parents. I ask myself, "What in heaven's name are they doing or not doing?" The parent has very often created this negative trait in their children. "Will you now do something and take responsibility?" I ask. Most parents, even when confronted, choose denial or irresponsibility instead of reflection. Does the negligent, lazy, or self-absorbed parent expect society, the law, the teachers or a social worker to fix the end results of sloppy parenting? These troubled youth are either role modeling parent behavior or trying unsuccessfully to cope with improper upbringing. In a bold statement, using the writing on the wall, I state, "Mothers need to get back to committed, whole-hearted mothering!" Daddies are not exempt.

A mother's presence, her devoted involvement, her home cooked meals and chocolate chip cookies, her bed time stories and the play time set aside for her children are what magical, childhood memories are made of. A mother's heart, so big, is where a child finds their refuge and solace.

A good home is an extension of that heart, filled with childhood delights such as aromas coming from the belly of the kitchen, sounds of laughter and chatter in togetherness, plenty of playtime, feelings of warmth, acceptance, inclusion and an unrushed lifestyle. I am not spinning a fairy tale here, this is an obtainable reality. Actually, it is a normal, caring home as it is meant to be. This is what a child needs to wake up to each morning and return to through memories when an adult. Even in old age these past realities sustain us as we forever return in thought to our mother's lap and to her loving ways.

It is tragic to see the epidemic of struggling children, products of divorce or neglect. School teachers see an increase in the suffering children daily, yet their hands are tied. The insecurities are apparent in the child who is neglected or is a human ping-pong ball going back and forth between Dad's house and Mom's house. Then there is the over tired toddler, still in diapers, being yanked out of bed at 6:30 a.m. on weekdays and plunked in a daycare by 7:15 a.m. What about the stressed child that is nearly the last to be picked up at pre-school at 6:00 p.m? They are then rushed through dinner, a bath and thrown into bed by 8:00 p.m. These scenarios are in step with a society that has come to ignore the importance of family time and home life. What a total disaster this hurrying and scurrying, this lifestyle on the run, and this shaky foundation of shattered households.

I know of a little girl of two and a half years of age. She has been in day care full time since her first birthday. She is prone to morning tantrums and difficult behavior because she is overtired and does not want to go to preschool. Her grandmother told me she sleeps at least three to three and a half hours at naptime on weekends due to her exhaustion. Both parents, aspiring materialists, work full time to pay off their fancy home. Mother also travels for work often. Nice people, but not astute parents. I could use a more bristling adjective than astute, but I choose to bite my tongue. These people just do not understand why their little one does not want to leave her mommy. After all, they say it is such a beautiful modern daycare! I await the backlash when this child becomes a teenager.

I present to you now a second story. A woman came to Canada with her family from Russia. Her daughter was three at the time. Mom found a job, in this land of great opportunity, that had her working 50–60 hours a week. She left at 7:00a.m. and returned at 7.00 p.m. Today, that child that was literally abandoned by Mom, is 34 years old and has been a severe drug addict since age 15. No rehabilitation has worked. She has announced more than once that she hates her mother. Need I say more as to why?

All children between birth and six years old prefer to stay in their familiar home environment playing stress-free at their mother's feet with a little friend dropping by a few times a week. This is their Utopia. I simply call it a normal lifestyle based on a common sense approach. It is a child's fundamental right to be given this environment of minimal stress. What is happening to modern woman's nesting responsibilities? What will be the repercussions? Are children supposed to raise themselves these days?

In the wilds of the animal kingdom a mother will kill off the weakest one in her litter. She knows that it will struggle needlessly and not survive when grown. Of course, I am not suggesting we do the same, but it is a tough world out there and we are churning out weakened, dysfunctional children that will turn into weak, dysfunctional adults burdening social services, hospitals, and creating adults that cannot cope in society. This is because children are often not the priority of parents in today's world. We have become exceedingly self-centered, irresponsible, money pre-occupied, too busy to parent or just too tired from running all day. I also feel that many have forgotten that their children are their prize possessions.

Stressed out parenting or self-absorbed parenting leaves little time to devote to children. Under these circumstances children feel abandoned or unwanted. This creates deep wounds. Permanent scars that will never heal become etched into their psyches. They cannot understand why their needs are not being met or are being ignored. Studies show that negative vibes coming from a frustrated or stressed out mom creates a "hostile feel" to mom. Due to this feeling that pushes the child away, confusion sets in because the child instinctually knows that this is unnatural. This leads to eventual symptoms of anxiety, depression, self-abuse and anger that evolves into hostility as they grow. Parents need to be completely present for their children as draining as this may be at times. The children will feel calmer and more reassured as a result. They will thrive.

"No man is poor who had a godly mother" (Abraham Lincoln).

Every mother mothers in her own unique way; there is no one way of "shoulds" or one example to follow. In our uniqueness of being we all will make mistakes, it is human nature. When we look back at our parenting time, it is hindsight and reflection that are the greatest teachers of life. "If only I knew then what I know now" are the type of thoughts that fill us as we stand back and take in our end results. I, in my devotion to my children, have made countless errors in judgment just because I was still learning about love actualized. My children were the catalysts for self-realization and self-change. I now thank them for having been so resilient while I struggled to grow into becoming a better person. However, the instinct to love and protect them made up for my mistakes.

It is only now, twenty-five and some years later, that I can say from life knowledge gained that if I could do it all over again I would think and act differently being more aware now of the delicate psyches of my impressionable children. We all trip up in our mothering. The one thing I can say confidently is that throughout my mothering years love was a constant. It poured from me, for I, as you, have this ability to be an ultimate nurturer. I encouraged this part of me to develop for I fully devoted myself to the role I chose at that time.

Love is security and children need only two things to ensure proper psychological development. One is the unimpeded flow of love in their direction, the other is a constant sense of security and protectedness. Both are given primarily by the very present mom.

Kids are resilient. Their flexibility allows them to get through rather unscathed the adult imperfections of their parents. To a certain degree they will dodge the bullets, but some damage is always done. If the parents put their hearts into raising their children, it is the love that will smooth over the errors. Mom's availability is a big part of unconditional caring, especially during the needy ages between birth and seven years of age.

After that there is a pull to develop other needs such as socializing more with peers and academic stimulus of the mind. Mommy's heartstrings are still very much felt as the child ventures into the outside school environment. Those heartstrings will continue to pull the child home again and close to the mother after a day out in the world until childhood is replaced by developed adolescence.

The opportunity to "love simply for the sake of loving" makes itself known in parenting. It is for that very reason that I arranged my life and profession to be able to experience this by being a very present mother. Today, I have moved into the background of my adult children's lives, yet my presence is still felt but more now as an observer.

I hope that when I say to you that we need to get back to some serious mothering that you do not feel that I am challenging your mothering methods. Rather, I am implying that until grade one and then some, a mother has to be totally accessible and very involved. A child psychologically feeds off the supply of love provided by the mother. It is like breast milk. It is not available if the mother is not fully there. The bottle is a poor substitute for the real thing, as is the daycare.

As I look back now, I realize that it was but a moment in time that I had the privilege of being the centre of my children's world. In a blink of an eye they grew up and pried themselves from my protective arms, but by then my work had been completed. I had showered them with my values, morals, higher wisdom, life lessons and steadfast support to equip them for the world. As their confidence grew their focus shifted away from the parents to an awaiting outside life teeming with unexplored possibilities. I am glad that I chose the role of homemaker instead of moneymaker for those few years, for in the end money is cold while an abundance of family memories keeps me warm and entertained at all times.

In praise of devoted moms, I give you the words of Abraham Lincoln:

"All that I am or ever hope to be, I owe to my angel, my mother."

# 3

# Childless Nurturers

When something is a need because it is programmed within us we are wise not to deny it. If, for example, I am musically inclined I should bring it to the forefront, otherwise I will live my life with an empty feeling. I have endless options. I can play a musical instrument, join a choir, sing in the shower, listen to music or take dance lessons. I can also buy season tickets to the symphony or become the conductor of a symphony to gratify an inner want. The urge to nurture is but another such need. Mothers are fulfilled in their parenting or grand parenting. Others, who are childless, must direct this inner energy elsewhere to satisfy it.

In esotericism, nurturer appears to be the key quality of the feminine principle on this plane. Protector is the key quality for the masculine. It would make sense that in the public sphere, women would want to express this need especially if in private life they were not mothering. Since it is a primary core force driving the female, it requires expression or it will implode as it builds up within her. The mental health consequences are then numerous as are physical manifestations of illness at some point in her life.

The deepest urge in males is based upon them being territorial. They protect that which is their own. It can be done in many ways without being physically aggressive, but as a core need it will be expressed in some fashion. Macho types, or real men as they prefer to be called, position themselves as the feared alpha dog. They tend to be more aggressive when protecting their family, jobs, home and belongings. The gentler male uses different methods, but is still protective by instinct just as females are nurturers by intuition.

Women are driven by a strong inclination to connect and care on a profound level. Their soulfulness, their abilities to support, aid and be peacemakers and healers are extensions of this core drive. We see their loving nature in their attraction to puppies and kittens, to a stranger's child in a stroller, to injured birds in their backyard and to charitable causes. This is positive energy for it originates in the heart mind. By using it continuously it moves outwards and expands. If we deny it, it turns stagnant and diminishes. In the end it becomes a negative, destructive force, souring within, creating problems both physical and psychological.

Luckily, women have numerous ways of expressing and keeping active this true nature even if they are not parents. They can become global mothers, or mothers for humanity instead. As I said, child bearing is a choice and with today's exploding population, I would not be surprised if women may soon decide that no children are preferable. It may just be a timely choice for in this troubled world of injustices women need to direct their energies towards creating change by nurturing society's woes instead.

There are many levels to do this on. After World War Two we saw women enter the business world mainly as assistants to men, as in nurses to doctors, secretaries to bosses, and general clerics in male run corporations. As women entered the work force they soon became college and university graduates in the 1960s and afterwards.

Let us look once again at the balanced world of polarity where two separate energies intermingle, retain their unique properties, and create a harmonious reality. How could this apply in the work world? Women come from a place of morals, ethical values, caring and the desire to help others. Much has changed for women in the workplace since the end of World War Two. They now have choices. If females without children focused upon professions that appeased an inner need to nurture, everyone would benefit. These types of jobs are just as important as male-oriented jobs.

There are certain types of work saturated with the female presence. That is because these jobs nurture others in some fashion and augment the energy of the woman. Women without children, or empty nesters, would be wise to consider these professions.

To nurture means such things as: to aid, heal, support, nourish, teach, rescue, minister to, counsel, lend a hand, nurse, relieve, cultivate, accommodate, help out, befriend, do service for, encourage, talk to, listen to, uplift, give to, and volunteer for. There are hundreds of meaningful jobs that require heart work and soul work and help support the feminine way. In her natural element woman would feel totally at ease pursuing a career that enhanced who she truly is.

On another level, there are no shortages of worthwhile endeavors to help improve society by tending to the needs of the less fortunate. These are charities, support groups, fundraisers, community projects, volunteer work, events organizing, animal and human rights projects and environmental causes for women to donate their hearts to.

Some, not that way inclined, choose instead to fuss over and nurture spouses, elderly parents, friends, nieces and nephews, cats, dogs or pet rabbits. Some foster children or are mentors. Others focus their nurturing on their magnificent gardens, on cooking and entertaining or on knitting scarves for everyone they know. The drive "to take care of" must always find an outlet.

Lastly, there is the good Samaritan nurturer. This woman extends herself over and over again by offering niceties to neighbors, co-workers, acquaintances and sometimes even to strangers. Most people refer to them as big-hearted individuals. These types of daily good deeds also fill this deep urge and are like a sprinkling of fairy dust, which magically makes life a pleasant experience for all that benefit.

A genuine nurturer does not come from "Tell me what to do

and I will do it." The person who leads with the heart notices on her own, time and again, that there is a need to be filled for another and just jumps right in with a random act of kindness. This is true woman's way. If she is not forced to restrict who she is capable of being, her nature radiates, generating feelings of warmth that embrace and coddle all around her.

If I can stop one heart from breaking
I shall not live in vain
If I can ease one life the aching
Or cool one pain
Or help one fainting robin into his nest again
I shall not live in vain
(Emily Dickinson)

# 4

# Spiritual Woman

As mentioned at the onset of this book, upon the shoulders of women lay the great task of setting things right, simply because of the properties that define her.

The earth is much older than scientists' current projections, so is humanity. In the archives of ancient knowledge where, as yet, few venture to glean information, it is revealed that through de-spiritualization, cruelty, conceit and greed, humanity's inharmonious energies have attracted to itself four global catastrophes. I am not referring to the documented ice ages or warming trends of natural climate change that were a part of the normal cycles and shaping of the earth's current geography. I am referring to man-induced disasters of global proportion that go back well over one hundred thousand years. As per these writings, a fifth, unnatural disaster is looming due to mistakes repeated.

Love is a core property of the feminine way and is a part of the plan that leads to humanity's recovery. Love enters the soul through spirit. To say that one is spiritual is to live by this law of love as our guiding light.

"To build character through our loving ways," as Aristotle would say.

Religion is not spirituality (not to be confused with spiritualism or spiritualists). Religions are merely stepping stones or the basis to spirituality, teaching us about Divine purpose and our higher natures.

Religions make us aware that spiritual thoughts are the seat of morality. Once we have been introduced to this, it is up to each one of us to spiritualize our thoughts, actions and attitudes, to move us towards revealing the possibilities of the beauty and glory within us. In the slow process of doing this, we gradually reach the point of a more spiritual and esoteric approach to life which is supportive and harmless to ourselves and those around us. This is the enlightened or loving frame of mind that is fed from a higher place and resists the animalistic, physical, self-indulgences that are fed by the lower ego's desires and self-pre-occupation creating indifference to others. One is simply from the higher expansive mind, the other comes from the lower, limiting mind.

For woman, one way to re-awaken your spirituality is by nurturing your natural connection to the feminine Divine energy within yourself and to listen to Her messages and direction. If nothing else just follow your intuition, it is Her guide.

This guides the female home to her centre which is the place that reminds her over and over again who she really is, lest she forget. Too many women already have forgotten through pre-occupation with the outside reality of illusions. We are becoming willfully ignorant for this inner draw is persistent, yet often we choose to deliberately dismiss it altogether. This is unnatural and therefore peculiar behavior indeed.

Who does not want to return to our home of origin when it beckons and welcomes with unconditional acceptance? Within our natures we have our physical, childhood home and in our soul selves we have our spiritual home or if you prefer the place we came from. Those who have experienced momentary death and have revived speak of a light and its feelings of comfort and peacefulness emanating towards them. This light of love and truth resides within the core of each of us, as well.

The feminine principle is very much a part of the composition of this inner anchor of reality that is made available to us at all times. We do not have to physically die to experience it, we simply have to periodically let go of the pre-occupations of the physical world and journey within to our abstract selves. Here is the platter of abundant insights, available for our taking, leading us more easily towards inner development and self-awareness.

"True loss is for him/her whose days have been spent in utter ignorance of the real self" (From the Divine Art of Living, a book of the Bahai Faith).

To be spiritual is quite easy for woman for it is one of her natural properties. She can also be religious, or both. To be neither is to be dead within or dead to herself. This tragedy of non-beingness affects all who are in close association with her.

The following are some indications that woman is living true to her nature. Basically, she celebrates her soul and its connection to higher truths. She takes time for her spiritual development. Primarily it is through her heart mind that she seeks answers to life's challenges and its mysteries. She embraces equality and unity. As well, she honors the Divine within her through her loving ways directed to all around her through an attitude of selflessness.

Love proclaimed, in its many forms, is spiritual truth exalted. Love stifled is this truth rejected. If the latter is allowed to take place within each of us then cold intellect easily dominates over the heart mind and becomes the wrongful master distorting our thoughts and actions. As woman de-spiritualizes, an imbalance in the world is created and a chilly, harsh reality sets in, the opposite of the collective sisterhood of unity mindedness.

"And now abides faith, hope and love, these three, but the greatest of these is love" (I Corinthians, chapter 13, verse 13).

As indicated in Chart A, woman is of soul passion expressing with ease the various types of soulful love. In so doing she helps spiritualize her surroundings. Through heart work she directs others back towards the light within themselves.

This is especially important now at the dawn of the Millennium of the Divine Mother. To usher in this transformational period, women need now to reach high into cosmic knowledge and deeper into heart wisdom. For it is written that there is no possibility of rescuing humanity if we bring upon ourselves a fifth and final global calamity. As long as we remain unfaithful to our higher natures we make this a greater possibility.

A woman's inner need is to live in accordance with her ancient feminine nature and stop grappling with the external standards set by masculine attitudes that are replacing her beliefs. The loss of her Divine Feminine side creates a great distress within her and yet this deeper wisdom can never be severed for it is immortal and is programmed into her. It is her duty to know these spiritual mysteries and hand them down to the next generation. Modern woman has all but forgotten the inner life for the disconnection is painfully obvious as she neglects her calling. Woman is intended to teach the art of Divine living by example and through the Word. She becomes a mentor, a role model when attuned to her inner self. She is here as well, to help her children to understand life's deeper journey, that personal conflicts are challenges that test the soul on its way towards spiritual maturity.

Woman's wisdom offers support to help soothe inner concerns, to develop healthy relationships and to find deeper purpose to life beyond fleeting pleasures. She is here to help us develop virtues that are the builders of self worth. By instruction and example she is the one to direct us towards prayer, meditation and quiet periods of contemplation (self-reflection). She teaches gratitude for life and for our personal life force. She is the imparter of ancient ways and mysteries that are the laws of the higher self. She encourages equality and unity mindedness and in it, humbleness and service to all in need. Through her ways and her guidance she creates a spiritual home for her loved ones and contributes a spiritual presence to the world. Is this the true woman that you are? If not, perhaps it is time to examine just how far you have strayed from the cosmic blueprint of real woman.

The innate needs to preserve, birth and transform drive the woman. She, therefore, has a preservation instinct to protect life as well as spiritual vision to foresee the consequences of wrong action. The spark of light within her heart speaks clearly to her and inspires her to be the dedicated catalyst of change and preservation. One does not hear from heart-minded women "Who cares what happens, we will all be dead in fifty years anyway." We do however, hear it from man's mouth, who is immersed in the lower mind of "me-indulgences" and concerned only about the immediate present.

The urgent mission of cosmic intelligence is to move all on the planet towards a more stable balance, a harmonic relationship between the masculine and feminine, long denied and long overdue. Positive change and improved realities are always the end result of the sacred marriage in equilibrium.

Let us now take a quick detour to once again prove this point. Many of you have heard of the spiritual third eye located in the middle of the forehead. This abstract eye, positioned between the pineal and pituitary, is that of perfected or complete vision. How do we open this third eye? The left and right brain possess the qualities of Charts A or B. Our two eyes are influenced by either the left or right brain, depending upon which is dominant in the individual. We see what we want to see according to that influence. When the two sides of the brain will work in balance coming together in a state of separate inter-beingness, a birthing of a whole new perception will occur. This is the awakening of the dormant third eye. This represents the balance of the physical realities with the spiritual realm.

"The eye of true vision is within the soul." (Gospel of Mary Magdalene).

The attainment of the third eye gives us greater "in" sight, and is an accomplishment earned from our individual choice to evolve. It is not simply given to us. It is one of the gifts attained by connecting to higher knowledge. Let us now return to spirituality of woman.

The Sacred Feminine is wise, merciful and emanates cosmic

love for all that is. Woman is programmed as an extension of Her to do the same. Here in the self-limiting, third dimension we do not seem to want to move out of, we are still somehow able to express love in varying intensities. There is love of our pets, of nature, of dear friends, of mates, of parents, of brothers and sisters, of our own children, self-love and the love of all that is, which is often intertwined with love of our Divine Creator.

The self-love I refer to is not the lower ego's need for self-gratification. It refers to one's personal pursuit of self-purification by continually focusing upon dissolving impurities of thought that lead to wrong action towards self and others.

There are greater and more intense forms of love and lesser or more superficial. For example, I love (desire) spaghetti, chocolate and a long massage, but not all together! These are all desire-based and for fleeting pleasure. However being one with nature or appreciating beautiful art forms moves the soul and is, therefore, a more profound and meaningful form of love. Love of one's children is deeper still and love of the God/Goddess is deeper yet.

Food for thought: In the esoteric teachings of the composition of words and the power in their vibrational soundings, the word "love" is the same word as "evolve." The identical letters appear in both, one is written forward, the other is its backward version. The last "e" and "v" are simply doubled in "evolve." One is sounded forward, the other backward, yet the vibrational composition emitted is the same. Interesting, no? The hidden mysteries are filled with these little eye openers for those with "eyes to see." To become unconditional love is to evolve.

Women used to draw their spiritual inspiration from historical Goddesses, for they represent woman's innate divinity and unseen powers. Some of the more known Goddesses are as follows: Sarasvati, of Hinduism, is the embodiment of inner, spiritual wisdom. Venus, of Roman origin, is the Goddess of all types of love. Kuan Yin, of China, is the great mother of compassion and mercy. Freya is the Norse Goddess of creativity. Diana, of the moon, is Roman and represents nature and spiritual intuition. Zorya, in Russian mythology, represents fertility. Ukemochi, of Japan, is representative of transformation, creating new from that which is old and no longer useful. Women's traditional rituals and rites of passage come from Juno of Rome. Oya from the Niger exhibits leadership qualities. Athena of Greece is known as the protector or spiritual warrior. Greece also gives us the earth mother Gaia who is the creator and sustainer of all life. There are many more.

Lastly, I would like to mention the Mother of all Goddesses, Isis of Egyptian origin. She represents fertility, death and rebirth. Through her magical powers she shows woman that she can create from herself anything she desires. Isis was considered the patroness of all women of early Egypt. Her powers spread from Egypt throughout the Roman Empire. Eventually Augustus Octavius "forbade" worship of her.

Yet, the female Goddesses remain extensions of the ultimate, androgynous being as a distinct half of the energy of creation. From my research these representations of femaleness seem to be categorized under five headings.

There is the Mother-nurturer figure. She is primary caregiver and is associated as well with fertility, and creating beauty in the world from either the womb or through soul expression. Then there is the Priestess figure. She possesses knowledge from the abstract, unknown realm. She brings unconscious truths into the conscious world in an attempt to heal, enlighten and balance. We then have the Lover figure. She represents love in all of its levels from deep and soulful to sensual and superficial. She also expresses love as harmony through the arts.

Next we have the warrior figure that conjures up visions of sword wielding amazons. This is inaccurate because she is benevolent. She does, however, come from great strength and conviction for she knows who she is. Her focus is upon service for the greater good. She is filled with courage.

The fifth is the Crone figure. She comes from developed intuitiveness and a sense of inner knowing. Due to her profound wisdom she exudes assurance through inner calm. She is also known as the Matriarch.

All of these aspects of Goddess force reside within woman. At varying times we are supposed to be her different faces. Through promptings from our spiritual nature we can once again become true to our diversified self.

It would be timely for modern females to return to resurrecting the mythological Goddesses and their practical and spiritual qualities. In so doing, they would re-acquaint themselves with the true woman within that is an expression of the Feminine Spirit awaiting recognition.

# 5

# Nature's Physician or Divine Physician

Modern medicine focuses upon treating a health problem by isolating a gland, organ or body system and bombarding it with inorganic pharmaceuticals to try to normalize the situation. As with most quick fixes, they may be immediately effective but short-lived. For acute conditions such as that once-a-year cold or inflammation, modern medicine can dramatically soothe symptoms until the body quickly heals itself. However, this approach for chronic conditions misses its mark, for no time is taken to examine the underlying, building problem. Removing sections of or the whole troublesome body part is not a viable alternative either, for dis-ease or dis-harmony will pop up elsewhere if not resolved.

The westernized approach to health is also referred to as mechanistic medicine. It shares the same root with "mechanics" and "mechanical." This would imply that the body is treated like machinery or a car.

This logical, scientific procedure or male way, works well in theory and practice when dealing with inanimate, manmade objects, for in these cases pieces and parts are mostly independent of each other; not at all so with creations of nature such as the body. For that which is cosmically designed is inter-active with its surroundings or other parts. We, therefore, need to look at the whole health state of an individual if we are to obtain lasting results with treatment. Often poor lifestyle choices, self-neglect, damaging attitudes and self-sabotaging behavioral patterns are at the root of many re-occurring acute or chronic health issues created by psychic distress. According to ancient systems of medicine, still intact in eastern cultures, a person is a body, a psyche, and a social personality. All are intertwined and affect one another.

Therefore, plying a person with synthetic drugs that are incompatible with our organic bodies cannot be the simple solution. In fact, the serious side effects can kill you. In ill-health cases, unless due to accident or birth defects, the whole picture of a person needs to be examined, not just the physical vital signs. Otherwise, re-occurring conditions or flare-ups will become permanent baggage as the body tries to inform you through pain and discomfort that you are creating an imbalance on some level of your being.

Our chronic illnesses that fill doctors' waiting rooms need not be a part of our lives to such an extent as it is today unless they are created by traumatic accidents or birth defects. Conditions such as arthritis, high blood pressure, diabetes, obesity, kidney ailments, gastro conditions, constant migraines and a host of other illnesses can be kept at bay with whole or "wholistic," natural medicine approaches known as the woman's way that dates back to ancient times. Her focus is the application of organic cures, her second focus is soul health, the restoration of one's moral and spiritual wellness.

It was only with the advent of the age of reason starting in A.D. 1600 that wholistic, natural procedures were stifled. This age saw the birth of modern science and with it, scientific, practical medicine that separated not only the mind and emotions from the physical body, but began using methods that also isolated one part of the body from the rest. This current, scientific, mechanical way of Western culture leans strongly towards the male mannerisms of doing things.

Let us now look at the two hemispheres of humanity known as male and female polarity regarding medicine. Mechanistic medicine is practical. It isolates the health issue as a part of separateness consciousness. This concrete way, focusing upon the action oriented energy of yang, encourages one to obtain quick results which is very important in health crisis intervention. The feminine healer perspective tries to comprehend the problem in its totality. It examines the situation on all levels of a person's being, or holistically, to get a complete picture as to the culprit behind the physical manifestation or dis-ease. The yin, abstract way, puts the pieces together emotionally, mentally, soulfully, as well as investigating lifestyle choices. This way is slower but more determined and brings with it more permanent relief when one is not in an immediate life-threatening situation.

The woman's way works wonders with chronic conditions as well as with acute conditions that re-occur too frequently like numerous colds, weekly migraines, ongoing indigestion, frequent muscle spasms, bouts of depression, energy drains and so on. It also works preventatively to help educate the patient to make right choices that respect their overall well-being, thereby curtailing illness not only physically but also emotionally.

Male, practical medicine is likened to the exact sciences such as mathematics, chemistry or physics that work with facts and a straight to-the-point approach that answers the question "how to very quickly" get results. Female, intuitive medicine is abstract, natural and observes behavior. The focus is upon the deeper question "why" this condition is manifesting. It is concerned with understanding the ailment's cause. A woman's techniques to well-being link everything together. What we have in these two polarities are instant solutions, often being Band-Aid therapy, versus deeper reflection. Both approaches, working hand in hand, are needed if we are to return to a balanced state of overall health and extinguish rampant illness that plagues humanity. For our bodies appear to be weakening.

(W)holistic medicine originates from the far east or ancient civilizations such as India. Today, in North America, it is referred to as naturopathic, alternative, or complementary medicine and offers non-invasive, natural treatments that encourage and stimulate the body's healing abilities. Basically, the belief is that when the body, mind and soul resonate in harmony we appear to be more resistant to disease and our recovery time is quicker. This is because one's spirit has an unlimited ability for self-healing from a cellular to subtle level.

Modern healers of the old way embrace this belief of ancient wisdoms that are often based on common sense, and they work towards gradual transformation through the re-creation of harmony throughout the patient. It is only through physical or psychological discomfort that we finally realize that we are living our lives in an imbalanced state that is mostly self-induced as a result of self-neglect. Healing of all aspects of self is simply clearing away negative debris that encourages us to make poor lifestyle choices that destroy health.

Today pharmaceutical corporations are the greedy, controlling giants behind the treatment of illness. Greedy, because they will not acknowledge natural cures, and lobby against them. Kitchen cures and all natural, therapeutic methods of the wise woman's ways are highly discouraged. These manipulating, self-serving corporations make sure they always have their foot in the door. They fund medical colleges and start brain washing medical students early on to push their products onto patients when they graduate.

If the truth be known, there are also many attractive carrot sticks offered to established physicians to entice them to use their wares. Sadly, many general practitioners have become no more than pill pushers today; a far cry from the involved family doctor who as little as forty-five years ago visited the bed-ridden at home. Often, they prescribed nothing more than chicken soup, cold compresses, bed rest and a well-aired bedroom for convalescing. Today, the ill patient sitting forever in a crowded waiting room filled with contagious disease is in and out of a general practitioners office in as little time as it takes to say "ahhh" and be handed a prescription.

This lopsided health system, overshadowed by the yang approach, is shameful. It is ineffective because it is often rushed, not thorough and coldly impersonal. The G.P. is the first line of medical care. Doctor means a person of great learning. Archaic definitions also include "someone that is a teacher or educates" and "one who heals through conscience and compassion." What a great joke that is. No time is taken to educate the patient on attitudinal or lifestyle changes or on self-help procedures to minimize re-occurrences of acute conditions or to reduce chronic pain naturally. I have noticed of late that often doctors are actually a tad arrogant or irritated if you ask too many questions so that you can help yourself take charge of your condition.

Nurturing and educating are two valuable tools that accelerate healing, neither of which are available in a doctor's office or during a hospital stay. Technological machines, impersonal hospital rooms, frazzled nurses and doctors that lack bedside manners are all a part of the matter-of-fact patriarchal approach to medicine or westernized health care. It focuses on practicality while sacrificing compassion and a soothing environment.

When we are weak and feeling vulnerable in sickness, we all need nurturing and niceties as well as remedies. Perhaps a little foot massage, fluffing up pillows, a cup of tea and a little encouragement are needed just as much as medicine from the drugstore. Women are overall healers. They are humanity's caregivers as well as intuitive and sensitive physicians.

These inborn traits make them excellent health care providers professionally or in the home. When a woman in the home is versed in natural cures she works magic in preventative, acute, chronic and recuperative health care. Most malaise is not of a critical nature and can be treated at home with a little knowledge and T.L.C., unless it becomes bacterial or life threatening.

Wise women of the past were well trained in natural approaches to health such as herbal concoctions, healing foods, and therapies such as massage, manipulation and energy balancing. The variety of skills and practical knowledge that were handed down to them made them very capable in the healing arts. Add to this their qualifications listed as per Chart A and their contributions to health maintenance and recovery were invaluable.

Sadly, it was these very women of "secret" knowledge that were amongst those targeted by the witch hunts in Europe I spoke of earlier. Had this senseless slaughter not happened perhaps all this wisdom and know-how would still be being passed down instead of it having been nearly annihilated. If this had been the case, our hospitals would not be bursting at the seams.

However, that which is unwavering truth or higher wisdom is indestructible. It prevails and resurrects itself as it is doing today. While the health system of man's making crumbles under overload and inefficiency, healers are popping up everywhere in North America. These learned, well-educated health providers follow the eastern approach of ancient healing, integrating it with the yang methods as needed.

Naturopaths, natural health consultants, homeopaths, osteopaths, herbalists, aroma therapists, reflexologists, energy workers, touch therapists, body workers, acupuncturists, reiki masters, art therapists, psychotherapists, soul counselors and a host of other natural health specialists are pushing hard for recognition. Sadly, the physicians associations and their partners, the pharmaceutical companies, are doing everything to block alternative treatments from rooting and working alongside yang medicine. All in the name of ego, dominance and money-making.

As well, various types of eastern meditations, jin shin do, yoga, quigong, sacred dance, tai-chi, body-mind-soul workshops and schools of natural medicine are all a part of the woman's way towards ultimate well-being and are infiltrating Western culture. For example, spiritual therapies such as bio dynamics are based upon the concept that our behavior and our habits should be in sync with the rhythms of nature and the cosmos. All of the above mentioned, as well as many other therapies of natural intent, focus on the same idea. Healers, or practitioners of holism, by balancing mind, body and soul with the aid of nature's wisdoms, are great spokespersons for this approach to sacred therapies that create self-harmony while boosting immunity.

The Greek philosopher, Plato, in his wisdom of 2,000 years ago boldly stated that medicine was beginning to pay too much attention to the physical body. He felt more attention needed to be directed towards the health of the mind, emotions and soul, which influenced greatly the physical well-being.

Once again, because the time is now, it is woman's birthright as well as her innate responsibility to fulfill her destined role in the healing arts, to impart the ancient ways that were effective. She is the teacher and physician in this area. The toxic medications being pumped into our bodies are poisoning our systems, just as all the inorganic pesticides, herbicides, toxic sprays and synthetic fertilizers are poisoning the waterways and landmasses of our planet. It is high time and basic common sense to return to resonating with nature and to work with her; our health depends upon it.

Of course, as science advances, it is a boon to have high-tech equipment in hospitals to diagnose problems, identify bacteria, confirm life-threatening illness, and provide aid in crisis health care. These inventions, without a doubt, are invaluable. However, hospitals should not be on overload with those who simply have common illnesses that have blossomed into real problems due to self-neglect or ignorance.

If women, humanity's gifted healers, would at least once again acknowledge this ability within themselves and return to educating themselves about basic health care, perhaps over time, hospital beds would not be spilling out into the corridors as we became masters of our health instead of victims of our ignorance. Women need once again to become the teachers of health and encourage others to take responsibility for their bodies.

As it sits today, the opposite is happening. Women have devolved into knowing practically nothing about overall, natural care of the body, treatment of minor ailments, chronic condition prevention and keeping our immune systems strong. Call it willful irresponsibility. We do not appear to care to investigate self-help methods as long as there is a pharmacy around the corner to poison our bodies. No one can be bothered to take the time to make right choices. They prefer the quick pill, any pill, to mask the condition, not cure it. One thing I do believe is this: "If you ignore your health, it will go away!"

We have become products of impatience and fast fixes. We do not take the time to respect the temple that houses the soul, which in turn, connects us to spirit that provides the vital force which gives us life through its abundance of energy. Interestingly enough, on a side note, people choose not to drive decrepit cars for they keep falling apart. So they keep leasing or buying new cars to prevent inconvenience. Yet, we shamelessly abuse our bodies knowing that in time they too will, as a result, become prematurely decrepit from neglect and fall apart. Knowing that we cannot trade them in, one would think that we would do everything in our power to keep them tuned up. Fanatics aside, most of us devote little time to our basic health, when it should be a major focus of our daily lives.

Perhaps, in part, this is due to woman having left her post as educator and doctor for her family, bewitched by the "no fuss" physician's pill. Apart from her coaching and guidance on health care and preventative measures, there is much to pass on regarding natural remedies that are often highly effective replacements for those synthetic pharmaceuticals with zillions of alarming side effects. Returning to the basics of medicinal herbs, healing teas, natural salves and poultices, heat and water therapies, foods that boost immunity and even simple body work techniques are all a part of the wisdoms of the natural healer innate in all females.

How dead is this invaluable knowledge in the modern, city woman? Very. Proper nutrition, physical activity, relaxation techniques, lifestyle, hygiene, attitudes, emotional balance, stress management, healthy relationships, spiritual sustenance, humor and creative outlets are also a part of pro-active health and should be primarily introduced by the mother or matriarch of a family as a part of the teachings of the school of life. Most of this information has gone by the wayside as ignorance now breeds more ignorance and brings with it dire results of epidemic proportions.

Life force, otherwise known as chi, prana, or pneuma wanes or its flow is impeded if we do not take good care of ourselves emotionally, mentally, physically and soulfully. This is ancient woman's way of practicing health. Man's way is pharmaceutical, and treats one aspect not whole health. Each method has its valued place. One cannot create imbalance by invalidating the other's approach as is happening today. We have been brainwashed to believe that the natural way is to be laughed at. We are fooling ourselves and are only partially informed. Excessive illness is everywhere due to one sided medical views. Once again, yin and yang wisdoms need to work together.

Women as nature or Divine physicians of old and true ways are able to right this imbalance if they choose, once more, to remember that which courses through their being. If woman but looks around at the sickly population, she has in good conscience, little choice but to start realizing once again that she must pick up from where she left off as a part of manifesting her total beingness. She is able to teach from that profound place of knowing, tapping into intuition as well as instinct. Humanity, in its blindness, wails that viruses are becoming stronger. Nonsense! It is our immune systems and general health that is weakening due to our ignorance and blatant disrespect for our bodies and nature's cures.

The healing arts, to me, is the most important knowledge

other than basic survival information for it protects the body and encourages longevity and vitality. Of course, the sciences have made tremendous gains in health care over the last fifty years. Yet, this approach does not provide the tenderness and caring needed that encourage our bodies to heal naturally. Women as healers and educators can lead us in that direction and once again become the link between ignorance and knowledge, illness and health.

As a Naturopath of the olden ways, I could talk volumes on the subject of organic ways to achieve stable health. This is not my intent here though. This fascinating knowledge is one thing to know. The self-disciplined application of it is another matter. You have to love yourself enough to want health as a part of the gifts you give yourself and put the work into attaining it.

In this section I am only trying to awaken a very important side of woman so she can take the steps to reinstate herself as natural physician to help minimize ill health. These abilities and skills as organic medicine woman and intuitive healer are as easy for her as writing musical scores were to Bach and Mozart.

# 6

# The Creative Self

What is it to be creative? Some of us are often, others are once in a while, and others appear to have little creative imagination.

Every day, in many ways, we are unconsciously creative, such as mixing and matching what we will wear to a social gathering to what we will plant in our flower gardens this spring. This section about the gift of creativity that women possess refers more to conscious creativity. It is about personal expression, an extension outward of the deeper self. Often it is not dependent upon any learning but upon our natural skills and talents that bring our unique soul creativity into the world.

When we tap into this creative intelligence that we all possess, it lifts us up into a higher consciousness, a purer place not tainted by everyday troubles. This is when life becomes more rewarding and gratifying.

Life is not about finding yourself; it is about constantly creating yourself." (G.B. Shaw). We need to express our inner gifts, the inner passions that allow us to remain impassioned with life. I am referring to tapping into a form of intelligence that is not reliant upon mental stimulus. The feminine, right-brain consciousness is the mother of all creativity. This is because imagination, which is only found here, is the origin of all creative potential. It is no wonder then that woman is constantly expressing many levels of creativity in her daily life, through decorating, gourmet cooking for a festive occasion, singing, dancing, artistic expression, making centerpieces for the table, sewing curtains, scrapbooking, writing poetry, and a million other expressions that do not rely on the analytical, left brain's involvement.

"Creativity is also a form of intelligence that is having fun."

(Albert Einstein).

This type of soul expression is one of pure beauty, reproducing the harmonies of the spheres. While some call it soul channeling, I call it soul song. This type of channeling is filtered through the right brain and is then expressed vis-a-vis our unique skills. It can be on a subtle or on a genius level. This need for universal intelligence to create finds one way to express itself through you the individual. It is meant to become conscious form if not blocked or ignored by you. This free-flowing energy produces a positive and relaxing experience. Sometimes it can be an exhilarating one that can only be explained as a natural high, which is exactly what it is!

Since woman is soulful, all types of creativity ooze from her. A female who announces that she is not creative is one who has become too manly in nature (too left brain) or is too pre-occupied with responsibilities that block this part of her.

To express our hidden, inner beauty is to reveal our soul to the world, the part of self that has evolved over time and gives us each our distinctiveness in the sea of common beingness. How we express our creativity and what we produce with it is what makes us original. The urge to be creative is one of the properties of the Feminine principle and is therefore found in Chart A. Bringing beauty and harmony into the world from the celestial spheres that the soul resonates with affects everyone around us in a positive way. It is like an individual pumping refreshing oxygen into the air; everyone benefits. If we realize that our creative projects make the world a more beautiful place, we may be encouraged to let our imaginations run free.

Too much left-brain activity makes us very one dimensional and it chokes out the creative intelligence of another side of ourselves. Creativity requires deep feeling and imagination only. For example, one can paint a painting of a bird step-by-step and reproduce what one sees on canvas. Or, in the words of the late *Robert Henri*, an American painter:

"Paint the flying spirit of the bird, rather than just its feathers."

That is intuitive creativity that flows from the higher self. There are many levels and many forms of this which enhances the creative person's life. Free expression liberates us from our self-imposed shackles even if it is for short periods of time, stops the bombardment of worry and wearisome thoughts and aids our well-being. It is this song of the joyful soul that knows no pain or suffering that helps neutralize the physical hardships that fill a person's world. It is a universal balm that soothes, and an energy that uplifts. It re-energizes the person it flows through.

Responsibilities, worries, stress and challenges fill our daily lives. The "to-do" list never seems to get shorter. All this eats into our creative time where we need to go time and again, to escape. This other side of our self is our salvation, for it balances our lives. Few of us are fortunate to live our lives through creativity alone, but never getting around to joyful self-expression, even if it is only on the weekends, is tragic self-neglect. It is being half-alive. In woman it is denying one of her core properties. This programming of self-denial goes back to the yang oriented school system I spoke of earlier. Ninety percent of the curriculum focuses upon left-brain development, and minimal attention is directed to creative courses. Often they are mere fillers or electives offered once a week as a token gesture to include them. From childhood on the person is encouraged to focus primarily on activities in life that feed the male, left brain.

As we over time, will evolve into being androgynous, both sides of the brain will be utilized in balance. Many levels of intelligence will develop as a result giving us broader perspectives and understanding. Spiritual wisdom and creative expression, properties of the right brain, will be important aspects of this development.

Women being right brain dominant, yearn to connect with the inner self. Women left free of crushing responsibilities or limitations that go against their human rights blossom into creative beings with little effort or encouragement.

Soul exercise is no less important than physical exercise. Perhaps it is abstract and unseen but it needs to be expressed to enhance our vital life force.

At different times in her life passages woman needs to address different properties of her core self such as her creative nature.

A few hours set aside weekly, allows the creative self to be liberated and to express its inner joy through the person's gifts, talents and imagination.

Creative self-expression reunites us with universal rhythm or rhythm of the core self. "Creative me" can be anything you want it to be at that moment. Negativity, grumpiness, bitterness, sadness, disillusionment, depression, illness, aches, pains, addictions as well as "life sucks" attitudes are in part, symptoms of creativity unexpressed, unheeded.

Nothing lifts me up faster than embracing my inner passions even if it is for forty-five minutes in my day. At this moment in my ever-changing life they include soul dancing in my living room, gardening and writing this book. Boring? Hardly. For me, it is deeply satisfying my soul. It also brings me to a place that releases the tensions of everyday responsibilities filling me with a more uplifting attitude.

Creativity is an inner need from the soul that wants to express itself outwards. It wants to become a more obvious part of your daily life to help strengthen identity as well as to enhance the mundane; for it is always a state of joy. It is its own form of intelligence.

The word *creation* brings with it words such as: constructive, achievement, fruition, genesis, birthing, developing, formative and generate. These words have a positive vibration to them.

If this is so, how is it then that we see around us creative expression that has dark and unsettling overtones to it? This is coming from negative attitude or unhealthy emotions, not from the inner well spring of the soul's pureness. It is necessary to differentiate between the two artistic displays. To hear the agitating, angry music of some young bands today does not exude beauty through harmony, but discord from its creator. This is not from soul expression, it is merely expression. We can go to an art gallery and see a modern painting that may be three vertical lines with two horizontal lines squiggled through it and label it artistic. Okay, but this too does not come from any deep place that resonates harmony and is not the soul creativity I speak of.

I recently went to a woman's home and the mom showed me her twenty-four-year-old daughter's university art project. It was a doll, mostly in black, who looked ravaged or mutilated. The expression was void of beauty. This is not art, rather it is a cry for help from trapped emotional pain or self-destructive thought forms.

In today's world, anything goes, so it seems, and everything is called art. However, creative expression speaks volumes of the inner state of the creator and their ability to access their inner joy, if they can at all. It allows us to check ourselves by examining our creations to see if we are expressing beauty, or if we are producing dolls dressed in black that come from a troubled place within us that overshadows the light within us.

Creativity, in healthy fashion, fans our vital life force, pumps us up when we feel deflated, and is somehow entwined in our life purpose of becoming the most we can be in this incarnation. Life offers us its canvas to improve, express and recreate ourselves on in any manner we choose.

"When you are inspired by some inner purpose, some extraor-dinary personal project, all your thoughts break their bonds. Your mind transcends limitation, your consciousness expands in every direction and you find yourself drawn into a new, great and wonderful world. Your dormant forces, creative faculties and talents come alive and you discover yourself to be a greater person by far than you ever dreamed yourself to be."

Patanjal Yoga Sutra (200 B.C.)

# 7

# In a Nutshell

In choosing to continue to live in the current state of separateness consciousness mindset, woman remains lost unto herself. It does not matter if she is living in a primitive tribal culture or is a C.E.O. of a large corporation. She still senses this unnatural state deep within.

An inner knowing keeps trying to re-direct woman to the source of knowledge that is programmed within her beingness. This knowing is as real as instinct and intuition and, if she acknowledges it, will make her destined journey back to her identity an easier path to follow. The spirit of love is the base of woman's true identity. Our Creator, or place of origin, is love. Woman is here to manifest it in its multitude of expressions.

Through the weaknesses of greed, self-centeredness, lust, gluttony, indifference, lack of conscience and morals, egotism and other non-loving traits inspired by separateness consciousness, we hurt ourselves and others, acting the complete opposite of our programming. We have fallen off the path that leads home to our true nature. For the most part, we ignore our higher minds or spiritual conscience that tries to direct us back to our origins.

As an advanced life form we are privileged indeed. Our minds have evolved to the stage where we can choose to raise ourselves up and tap into expansive consciousness and be privy to unifying cosmic truths that influence all universal life. Or, we can descend further into our lower egos. In so doing, we will abase ourselves to the lowest of life forms that are so preoccupied with the needs of self that it will continue to lead us further into wickedness and cold-heartedness, culminating in savagery or acts of the beast.

The highest consciousness encourages us to live in a

courteous, kindly manner, respecting all life and leads to a more blissful existence. The lowest consciousness encourages corrupt beings, abusive, and uncaring people with no conscience and therefore no boundaries. Often the acts of these people are appalling, incomprehensible and inexcusable. We are here to evolve into emissaries of love and selflessness and have unlimited capacity to do so. Somehow, I strongly feel that it is the collective Feminine Divine re-awakened in women that will direct us back upwards and halt this downward spiral.

Humanity's unimpeded descent further into the lower mind brings with it endless atrocities toward one another supported by indifference. Becoming soulless is accelerating this nosedive. True woman comes from a deep place of higher wisdom that can lead us back to that spirit of love within us that exhibits genuine caring. Woman's energy, as shown in the properties of Chart A, is truly the ideal partner in the sacred marriage of soul reality of higher mind with physical reality of lower mind. This is the crucial balance needed between male and female.

All answers, all information, all direction we seek lie within. Through the woman's way we need to tap back into and materialize these foundational truths.

Without preference or prejudice, simply from a lifetime of observing humanity, studying esoteric truths and from an inner intuition, I know it is high time for the Goddess to re-birth in every woman as a way of re-connecting her to cosmic intent. So ladies it is up to you now. Do your part, cock an ear and really listen to Her whisperings, all the while opening your hearts to Her cosmic energy and your wombs to Her creative seed.

# 8

# These Closing Lines

At eighteen years of age, on the cusp of young womanhood, I wrote my first poem entitled "Who am I? Why am I? Where am I?" I went on to write many other soul searching bits of poetry in my twenties and thirties All of them I still have except this first one which I lost over twenty-five years ago. It remains in my heart haunting me. Yet, interestingly enough, I do not remember any of the words except for the title.

As I now write these final pages, I realize that this lost poem was intended to lead to this book. At eighteen, I may have lamented through this piece of poetry as I was yet unable to answer these profound questions. Now I can, and so I will in these closing lines.

As long as I thought that in my attitude of separateness consciousness I was modeling after the Divine Feminine within me, I remained disconnected to Her true essence. It is only when I realized that I was not a complete representation of Her, that I surrendered separate consciousness and merged back into Her. I can now, as a result, answer the question, "Who am I?"

I finally took notice that in this time frame which I was born, the Cosmic Feminine is reaching out to every woman to act upon and rectify Her pain of neglect. This imbalance, needing to be adjusted, helped me answer the question, "Why am I?" Women are one with Her. Due to this interconnectedness I now know that I can make a positive difference and help make Her voice heard.

Through a lifetime devoted to the pursuit of inner wisdom, I opened my heart to life around me. I developed respect, acceptance and compassion for all that is. From this I realized that we are all on the same journey and because of that we are all universally one. This insight allowed me to answer the question,

"Where am I?" Simply, I AM. No airs. I AM a part of all that is. That is where I belong and that is where you will find me; connected, involved, and caring.

Joyfully from the light within
Corinne

"KNOWING WHO YOU REALLY ARE AND HONORING THAT SELF REMOVES ALL MISERY AND MOST SUFFERING."

# Butterfly Woman

In mythology and nature spirituality the butterfly is the power animal associated with transformation and metamorphosis. It symbolizes breaking through our self-imposed limitations raising ourselves up to a higher consciousness, a greater awareness. Often it is associated with deep spiritual transformations on the continual journey of self-discovery.

The butterfly reflects a sense of joyful freedom as it continually changes. Change at times is a lengthy process but the rewards are worth it.

Butterflies breaking free of the cocoon represent the release of ourselves from that which holds us entrapped, liberating into this world the inner or soul self. It is dismantling negative programming, crippling emotions and fears that are etched into our psyches. In Greek the word psyche means soul but it also means butterfly.

We are destined to be constantly evolving, moving forward, growing and becoming. It takes courage to emerge from that cocoon that we encase ourselves in over our lifetime.

Women of the world break free, crumble your cocoons. It is time to test your wings. *No time left to delay*. Have confidence, go forth, catch the wind of spirit and soar. Share your wisdom and potential with a world that patiently awaits your metamorphosis back to the *true* self.

# Seven Pearls of Wisdom

1. Know thyself as a manifestation of God/Goddess.
   This is awareness.

2. Realize and develop your potential.
   This is self-discipline.

3. Reject separateness. Remove personal boundaries created
   by desire, want and gain.
   This is unity mindedness.

4. Practice moderation in all things.
   This is balance.

5. Harm nothing, no one, not self.
   This is love.

6. Remain connected, yet detached from outcomes.
   This is freedom.

7. Express joyfulness through productivity.
   This is service to the race.

# Chart A

Cosmic Blueprint of Some Feminine Properties

A. Associated with nature (natural laws of the universe)

B. Benevolent, tolerant

C. Connects to soul wisdom (abstract, inner reality)

D. Emotional (operating with acute sensitivity, feeling)

E. Passive

F. Intuitive

G. Nurturer

H. Connected to the collective unconscious (soul, higher ego)

I. Healer

J. Responsive, giving

K. Peace maker, non-confrontational

L. Discreet

M. Flexible and yielding

N. Gatherer

O. Empathic

P. Tender, supportive, gentle

Q. Cautious and conservative

R. Contractive

S. Ecologically conscious

T. Sensual, relationship oriented

U. Open to receiving nurturance

V. Identified with the moon's energy

W. Associated with negative pole

X. Receptacle, stillness

Y. Circular, cyclical and infinite

Z. Creative

# Chart B

Cosmic Blueprint of Some Masculine Properties

A. Associated with lower mind (manmade laws)
B. Authoritative, dominating
C. Connects to the outer life (concrete, physical reality)
D. Rational (operating through reason and logic)
E. Active
F. Intellectual
G. Protector
H. Connected to the separate consciousness (lower ego)
I. Provider
J. Indifferent, taker
K. Warrior, seeks confrontation
L. Direct
M. Structured and competitive
N. Hunter
O. Assertive (or aggressive)
P. Strong, controlling, bold
Q. Risk taker and progressive
R. Expansive
S. Self over environment
T. Athletic, goal oriented
U. Self-reliant
V. Identified with the sun's energy
W. Associated with positive pole
X. Penetrator, movement
Y. Linear and finite
Z. Practical

# The Intent

I am me, while you are thee
enveloped all in unity
a pulsating global family
in the universal "one"

Wisdom clears my eyes to see
that "collective" is a part of me
separateness can never be
in the universal "one"

To cosmic order I belong
cosmic rhythm rises into song
harmonizing us along
in the universal "one"

Energies of each polarity
two halves of a totality
one is that of womanity
in the universal "one"

Distinct poles of a collective sea
Embrace in a sense of unity
The source of celestial melody
the intent ...
of the universal "one"
CORINNE CARMEN

"LOVE AND KINDNESS ARE THE BASIS OF ALL SOCIETIES. IF WE LOSE THESE FEELINGS THE SURVIVAL OF HUMANITY WILL BE ENDANGERED"
*The Dalai Lama*


"ONE WORD FREES US OF ALL THE WEIGHT AND PAIN OF LIFE:
THAT WORD IS LOVE"
*Sophocles*

"THE HEART IS THE CHILD OF THE UNIVERSE'S SOUL"
*Corinne Carmen*

# Interesting Books

| | |
|---|---|
| Anastasia | Megre, Vladimir |
| A Woman that Glows in the Dark | Avila, Elena |
| A Woman's Worth | Williamson, Marianne |
| | |
| Aquarian Gospel of Jesus Christ | Levi |
| Born to Love | Leo Buscaglia |
| At the Root of This Longing | Flinders, Carol Lee |
| | |
| Book of Shadows | Curott, Phyllis |
| Care of the Soul | Moore, Thomas |
| Egyptian Gods and Goddesses | Hart, George |
| Embracing Our Essence | Skog, Susan |
| Embracing the Goddess Within | Waldherr, Kris |
| Finding Meaning in the Second Half of Life | Hollis, James |
| Grand Mother of Light | Gunn-Allen, Paula |
| Herbal Healing and Spirit Healing the Wise Woman way | Weed, Susan |
| Igniting Intuition | Northrup, Christiane |
| | |
| Isis | Blavatsky, Helena |
| Isis in the Ancient World | Hopkins, John |
| Mary Magdeline, Myth and Metaphor | Haskins, Susan |
| Mother Earth Spirituality | McGaa, Ed |
| MotherWit Child, | Mariechild, Diane |
| PaGaian Cosmology | Livingstone, Glenys |
| | |
| Sacred Circles | Craig, Sally |
| Substance of Thought | Beasley, R.P. |
| The Basic Ideas of Occult Wisdom | Winner, Anna Kennedy |
| | |
| The Body of the Goddess | Pollack, Rachel |

| | |
|---|---|
| The Chalice and the Blade | Eisler, Riane |
| The Feminine Face of God | Hopkin, Patricia |
| The Finding of the Third Eye | Stanley-Alder, Vera |
| The Fifth Dimension | Stanley-Alder, Vera |
| The Goddess Re-Awakening | Nicholson, Shirley |
| The Lost Gospel of the Earth | Hayden, Tom |
| The Mists of Avalon | Zimmer-Bradley, Mario |
| The Power of the Goddess in Ancient Egypt | Roberts, Alison |
| The Secret Teachings of Mary Magdalene | Nahmad, Claire |
| The Seven Sacred Rites of Menopause | Meisenbach-Boylan, Kristi |
| You Own Your Own Power | Altea, Rosemary |
| You the Healer | Kramer, H.J. |
| Woman as Healer | Achterberg, Jeanne |
| When God was a Woman | Stone, Merlin |
| When Humanity Comes of Age | Stanley-Alder, Vera |

AXIS MUNDI
BOOKS

Axis Mundi Books provide the most revealing and coherent
explorations and investigations of the world of hidden or
forbidden knowledge. Take a fascinating journey into the realm
of Esoteric Mysteries, Magic, Mysticism, Angels, Cosmology,
Alchemy, Gnosticism, Theosophy, Kabbalah, Secret Societies and
Religions, Symbolism, Quantum Theory, Apocalyptic
Mythology, Holy Grail and Alternative Views of Mainstream
Religion.